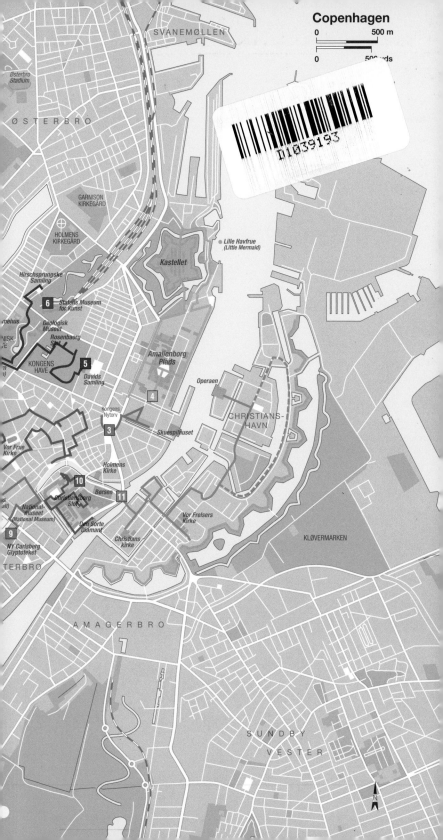

Copenhagen

0   500 m

0   500 yds

SVANEMØLLEN

Østerbro
Stadium

ØSTERBRO

GARNISON
KIRKEGÅRD

HOLMENS
KIRKEGÅRD

Kastellet

Lille Havfrue
(Little Mermaid)

Hirschsprungske
Samling

6 Statens Museum
for Kunst

Geologisk
Museet

Rosenborg
Slot

NISK
E

KONGENS
HAVE

5

Davids
Samling

Amalienborg
Plads

Operaen

4

Kongens
Nytorv

3

CHRISTIANS-
HAVN

Skuespilhuset

Vor Frue
Kirke

Holmens
Kirke

10

Børsen

11

Christiansborg
Slot

Vor Frelsers
Kirke

National-
museet
(National Museum)

Den Sorte
Diamant

9

Christians
kirke

KLØVERMARKEN

NY Carlsberg
Glyptoteket

TERBRO

AMAGERBRO

SUNDBY

VESTER

N

INSIGHT GUIDES

COPENHAGEN

StepbyStep

APA PUBLICATIONS L

Part of the Langenscheidt Publishing Group

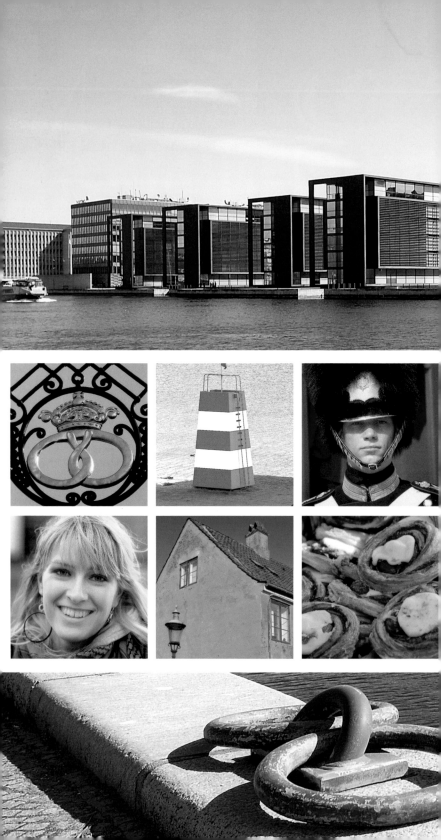

CONTENTS

ABOUT THIS BOOK

Above: some of the attractions of Copenhagen.

This *Step by Step Guide* has been produced by the editors of Insight Guides, whose books have set the standard for visual travel guides since 1970. With top-quality photography and authoritative recommendations, this guidebook brings you the very best of Copenhagen in a series of 14 tailor-made tours.

WALKS AND TOURS

The tours provide something for all budgets, tastes and time spans. As well as covering Copenhagen's classic attractions – of which there are many – the routes track lesser-known sights, and there are also day excursions for those with both the time and inclination to explore slightly further afield.

The tours embrace a range of interests, so whether you are an art enthusiast, an architecture buff, a gourmet, a lover of flora and fauna, a historian or royalist, or have children to entertain, you will find an option to suit. For our pick of the walks by theme, consult Recommended Tours For... *(see pp.6–7)*.

We strongly recommend that you read a tour before setting out. This should help you to familiarise yourself with the route and enable you to plan where to stop for food – options are shown in the 'Food and Drink' boxes, which are recognisable by the knife and fork sign, on most pages.

ORIENTATION

The tours are set in context by this introductory section, giving an overview of the city, plus information on food and drink, shopping and entertainment. A short history timeline in this chapter highlights the key events that have shaped Copenhagen over the centuries.

DIRECTORY

Supporting the tours is a Directory chapter, comprising a user-friendly, clearly organised A–Z of practical information, our pick of where to stay and select restaurant listings. The entries grouped under 'Restaurants' complement the more low-key cafés and eateries that feature within the tours, and are intended to offer a wider choice for evening dining.

The Author

Antonia Cunningham was educated at Cambridge University, where she studied Languages and Art History. She has written several books, including non-fiction for children, two books on world art and the Impressionists, and five on Copenhagen and Denmark, including Insight's *Smart Guide Copenhagen*. She lives in London with her partner Nick and son Benjamin, to both of whom she dedicates this book.

This edition was revised and updated by Fran Parnell, whose passion for Scandinavia began while studying Norse and Celtic at Cambridge University. She has written guides to Iceland, Sweden, Denmark and Scandinavia.

Margin Tips
Shopping tips, handy hints, information on activities, key historical facts and interesting snippets help visitors make the most of their time in Copenhagen.

Feature Boxes
Notable topics are highlighted in these special boxes.

Key Facts Box
This box gives details of the distance covered on the tour, plus an estimate of how long it should take. It also states where the tour starts and finishes, and gives key travel information such as which days are best to do it or handy transport tips.

Route Map
Detailed cartography shows the tour clearly plotted with numbered dots. For more detailed mapping, see the pull-out map slotted inside the back cover.

Food and Drink
Recommendations of where to stop for refreshment are given in these boxes. The numbers prior to each restaurant/café name link to references in the main text. On city maps, restaurants are plotted.

The € signs at the end of each entry reflect the approximate cost of a three-course meal for one, without wine. These should be seen as a guide only. Price ranges, also quoted on the inside back flap for easy reference, are as follows:

€€€€   over 550dkk
€€€   400–550dkk
€€   250–400dkk
€   under 250dkk

Footers
Those on the left-hand page give the tour name, plus, where relevant, a map reference; those on the right-hand page usually show the main attraction on the double page.

SHOPPERS

Resist temptation in the department stores on Strøget (walk 2) and Kongens Nytorv (walk 3), the boutiques off Strøget, in Nørrebro (walk 7) and the independent artists and designer shops in Vesterbro (walk 1).

RECOMMENDED TOURS FOR...

DESIGN COPENHAGEN

Lap up serious modern design at Illums Bolighus on Strøget (walk 2). The Radisson Blu Royal is a design icon (walk 1) and Designmuseum Danmark has wonderful displays (walk 4).

FOOD AND WINE

Copenhagen has nine Michelin-starred restaurants. Værnedamesvej (walk 1) is Copenhagen's gourmet food street, while Magasin du Nord (walk 3) offers an excellent food hall.

CHILDREN

Treat the kids to a trip to Tivoli (walk 9), day or night, and fascinate them at the zoo (walk 8), Experimentarium (walk 13) or Bakken and the Akvarium (tour 14). Dazzle them at Rosenborg and visit the crown jewels (walk 5).

PARKS AND GARDENS

You can't come to Copenhagen, especially the first time, without experiencing the amusement park Tivoli (walk 9). On a sunny day, take a break in Kongens Have (walk 5), Frederiksberg Have (walk 8), Assistens cemetery or along the reservoirs (walk 7).

HANS CHRISTIAN ANDERSEN

Wander through his stamping ground around Kongens Nytorv and Nyhavn (walk 3), and visit the Bakkehuset (walk 1). See *The Little Mermaid* (walk 7) and visit the cathedral where his funeral was held (walk 2) and his grave (walk 7).

ART ENTHUSIASTS

You are spoilt for choice with the National Gallery of Art (walk 6), the Ny Carlsberg Glyptotek and the National Museum (walk 9), the Thorvaldsens Museum (walk 10) and Rosenborg (walk 5). Outside the city are world-class galleries Arken, Ørdrupgaard and Louisiana (tour 14).

CHRISTIAN IV AND THE RENAISSANCE

Visit Rosenborg Castle (walk 5), the Round Tower, Trinity Church and Caritas Fountain (walk 2), Børsen (walk 10), Kastellet and Nyboder (walk 4), Christianshavn (walk 11) and Frederiksborg Castle in Hillerød (walk 5).

ROMANTIC COPENHAGEN

Take a stroll along the reservoirs (walk 7), wander through Christianshavn (walk 11) or head along the banks of the Sound (walk 4).

ROYALISTS

Follow in the steps of kings at Slotsholmen (walk 10), Rosenborg (walk 5), Church of Our Lady Cathedral (walk 2), Amalienborg (walk 4) and Roskilde (walk 12). For a little royal shopping, visit Royal Copenhagen on Strøget (walk 2).

ORIENTATION

An overview of geography, customs and culture, plus
illuminating background information on food and drink,
shopping, entertainment and history.

OVERVIEW

Copenhagen is a pretty seaside city with a thriving nightlife, the sophisticated gastronomic and cultural offerings of a far larger city and a visible history going back 900 years. It supports plenty of big business and the world's third richest city in terms of gross pay per capita.

Population Density
Denmark is the smallest yet most densely populated nation in northern Europe with a land area of just 43,000 sq km (16,630 sq miles). In Denmark there are over six times as many people per sq km as in neighbouring Sweden.

Copenhagen (København), the capital of Denmark, is located on the eastern side of Sjælland (Zealand), the largest of Denmark's 407 (named) islands, with only the Øresund (Sound) separating it from Sweden. It was founded by Bishop Absalon in 1167, and these days, including its greater metropolitan area, is home to about 1.2 million of the country's estimated 5.60 million people. The smaller municipality of Copenhagen – made up of 15 districts that extend beyond the geographical scope of this book – accounts for approximately 625,000 inhabitants.

STRATEGIC LINK TO EUROPE

Connected by the south of Jutland to Germany, Denmark is the only Scandinavian country physically joined to the European mainland and, as such, is the bridge between Scandinavia and the rest of the continent. It is also literally the bridge to Sweden with the Øresund road and rail bridge linking it with the city of Malmö.

Consequently, Denmark shares many of the characteristics of its Nordic neighbours: liberal welfare benefits coupled with a high standard of living, and a style of government

that aims at consensus and the avoidance of petty bureaucracy. Yet Denmark is also more 'European' and accessible than the rest of Scandinavia, and its appeal is universal.

THE CITY

With its strategic location at the mouth of the Baltic Sea, Copenhagen has always been an important hub and, as such, a tempting prize for pirates and traders. As a small fishing village in the 12th century, it attracted the protection of Bishop Absalon and the dastardly attentions of Wendish pirates. One century later, German traders of the Hanseatic League were pounding on its doors. By the 15th century, the Sound was even more of a cash cow with its herring salted and exported all over Europe and the king charging a toll on every ship that passed on its way to the Baltic.

Over the centuries, Copenhagen grew but always, even today, remained reasonably compact, its residents moving out gradually from the central conurbation. In the 12th century, Slotsholmen was the centre; by the Middle Ages, the town had expanded across the water to the banks of what is now the Old Town.

The medieval citizens put up walls surrounded by a moat, which enclosed the city to the north, east and west. With the exception of Østerport (East Gate), which stood on Gothersgade until the 17th century, near to what is now Kongens Nytorv, the gates in the walls were on or near the sites still called Nørreport (North Gate) and Vesterport (West Gate). The fortress of Slotsholmen and the watery boundary of the Sound stood to the south. The five reservoirs to the north are all that remain of the medieval moat.

In the 16th century, under the aegis of Christian IV, the city's fortifications were extended east. The fortress Kastellet *(see p.52)* was built, and the East Gate and rampart moved up near it, thus bringing Rosenborg (1606–34) within the walls and practically doubling the amount of space inside the city walls in what was known as 'New Copenhagen'. To the south, Christianshavn *(see p.82)* was built up and a series of new islands created with naval yards and protective bastions. Nyboder, near Østerport, was built to house the naval workers. At the same time, Christian IV created some of the most lasting buildings of the entire city; boasting an elegant Renaissance style, they are still standing today.

One century later, the city expanded again, as Frederiksstad *(see p.47)* was built in 'New Copenhagen' on the land acquired by Christian IV. It was (and is) the most aristocratic area in town, and was constructed on the site of a former royal country palace that had burnt down. On the banks of the Sound, Kongens Nytorv was developed and Nyhavn was excavated and the merchants built their houses along its wharfs, to be close to the precious goods in their warehouses.

Fire was always a threat in a town made of wood, and the 18th century saw two shocking blazes that destroyed almost the whole of the medieval centre. With the odd exception (including, fortunately, most of Christian IV's marvellous buildings), what the visitor sees today is 18th-century neoclassical architecture.

By the 19th century, Copenhagen was too compact: it was packed with people and had no sanitation to speak of; certainly not enough to deal with the effluence that the heaving city spat out daily. In 1853, cholera broke out, killing several thousand people, including the well-known Golden-Age artist, Christoper Eckersberg.

In 1856, the old ramparts were pulled down to improve conditions and the populace spread into the countryside, which soon became the

Above from far left: Søndre Frihavn, north of the city; royals from all over Europe turned up for the wedding of Crown Prince Frederik with Mary Donaldson in May 2004.

Café Culture
Sitting out in a café is an indisputable part of the modern Copenhagen experience, but Copenhagen's first continental-style café, Café Sommersko, did not open until 1976.

Below: buzzing cafés in front of the multicoloured houses in Nyhavn.

Above from left: the unmistakable façade of the Palads Teatret cinema, in Axeltorv; Danes are keen cyclists; the city is dotted with beautiful, peaceful gardens.

districts of Nørrebro, Vesterbro, Østerbro and Frederiksberg (although this is still technically a separate municipality from Copenhagen).

Thanks to the architect and town planner Ferdinand Meldahl (1827–1908), these districts were conserved as the parks that ring the inner city today, stretching from Kastellet, via Østre Anlæg behind the National Gallery of Art, the Botanical Gardens and Ørsteds Parken. Tivoli, also once part of the ramparts, was the work of entrepreneur George Carsten in 1843 *(see p.75)*.

COPENHAGEN TODAY

The 20th and 21st century have seen further changes to the city. The old quarter was pedestrianised from the 1960s; the docks are being rejuvenated; and the authorities have taken a particular interest in updating the city's landscape with startling modern buildings such as the Black Diamond (1999), the Opera House (2005), the Royal

Below: sailing out of the harbour.

Danish Playhouse (2008), the DR Koncerthuset (2009), and the Blue Planet aquarium (2013). A whole new 'downtown' area, Ørestad, has been created from scratch on Amager island, and other areas of the suburbs are undergoing huge regeneration. Another ambitious project is the expansion of the Metro. The circular Cityringen line, made up of 15.5km (93 miles) of track with 17 new city-centre stations, is due to open in 2018.

Copenhagen Districts

As in most large cities, different areas can be categorised by the sort of people (and incomes) that tend to populate them. Indre By, the inner city covering an area of 8.98 sq km (2,200 acres), has a population of *c.*48,000. The quietest part of the Old Town is the financial district behind Kongens Nytorv and Holmens Kanal, where fewer than 500 live – there are generally more visitors gently snoring away every night than there are locals. More than half the apartments in this area are lived in by affluent young singles. They're also popular with those in the 50-plus age bracket, who want to be close to the city centre's cultural opportunities.

Students and young families tend to live in Nørrebro or Vesterbro, which are also Copenhagen's most multicultural areas. Nørrebro has a population of just over 74,000 and is the most densely populated district. In recent years, it has seen more social problems than other parts of the city; nonetheless, it has the reputation for being a cool place to hang out. Once-seedy

Vesterbro is now respectably edgy: over the last few years, a young, creative crowd has moved in and transformed the old meat-packing district, Kødbyen, into a hub of stylish new bars, clubs, restaurants and galleries.

Christianshavn is Copenhagen's little Amsterdam, surrounded by water; according to one commentator, it was 'built for rich people, taken over by poor people and is now radical chic', although there are plenty of affluent newcomers, resented by the locals, who are attracted by its regeneration.

Østerbro and Frederiksberg are more upmarket; there are several embassies in Østerbro, including those of the US, Canada, Great Britain and Russia.

AN ECO-FRIENDLY CITY

These days, Copenhagen is still a compact city and, for the visitor, eminently walkable or bicycle-friendly. The Danes cycle in their thousands: men in suits, mums with babies in cart extensions, people cycling with pets, as well as the students and the younger generation. It makes for a city with clear air, few traffic jams, an impression of safety and a satisfying sense of doing something for the planet, which plays a large part in most Copenhageners' psyche.

Being eco-friendly is no idle desire; 36 percent of people cycle to work, and there are 350km (217 miles) of bike paths with more planned. Special carriages for bikes on trains enable cyclists to combine biking with travelling on public transport more easily.

The emphasis on being eco-friendly becomes clear fairly quickly, from the wind farms in the Sound (incidentally, awarded a Blue Flag and clean enough to swim in), visible as you fly in to the airport or look up the Sound from the Little Mermaid, to the bikes and organic revolution that is taking place in Copenhagen's restaurants. The authorities are very active: they have decreed that 90 per cent of all food served in the city's public institutions will be organic by 2015, and that all citizens will be able to walk to a park in under 15 minutes. Copenhagen also has a very ambitious programme of recycling, with plans to limit non-recyclable materials to two per cent of household waste.

Wind Farms
The Middelgrunden wind farm on the Sound was the world's biggest when it opened in 2000. Turbines supply 19 percent of all Denmark's electricity.

The Danes

Copenhagen's inhabitants are as appealing as their city; liberal, generally law-abiding, socially responsible (just look at their generous social security system, paid for with huge taxes that no-one seems to complain about), gregarious, and – at the same time – charming and sarcastic. They are skilled at enjoying life, especially when it comes to enjoying *hygge*, a word that loosely translates as a combination of warmth, well-being and intimacy, usually involving the combination of family, friends, food and copious amounts of alcohol. They are also informal in dealing with people and put a lot of focus on their personal freedom.

FOOD AND DRINK

Thirty years ago, a trip to Copenhagen may not have yielded significant gastronomic pleasure unless you were keen on herring. That has changed and Copenhagen boasts the most Michelin stars of any city in Scandinavia.

The Local Hooch
Aquavit *(akvavit)*, the local spirit that is usually flavoured with caraway seed, is cheaper than imported spirits.

Traditional Danish food, as you would expect from a seafaring nation in a cold, murky climate, was based around sturdy, filling dishes of carbohydrates, meat and fish.

A generally agricultural and seafaring nation, people produced food from what they grew themselves or was available locally, using ingredients such as apples, beer, bread, cereals, carrots, dairy products, pork, onions, plums, potatoes and seafood. Dishes were seasonal in spring and summer but in the long, cold, dark winters, dishes depended on ingredients that had been preserved from the harvest seasons, using techniques such as pickling and salting. In the days of no refrigeration, it was these foods – ones that could be stored almost indefinitely – that came to dominate the fleeting pleasures of fresh fruit and vegetables, which barely feature in traditional dishes.

These days, Danish food, especially in restaurants, has lightened up. With more contact with foreign cultures and food through holidays, immigration and greater food marketing and availability, the Danes, like the inhabitants of much of the rest of Europe, have become increasingly familiar with foreign dishes and ingredients. Leading the way is a generation of young chefs who are grasping the opportunity to combine Danish dishes and flavours with ingredients from abroad to create a new 'fusion' cuisine (especially French, Italian and Thai), so producing a new angle and perception of traditional food from different cultures. There is also an ever-increasing emphasis on seasonal, fresh and oft-times organic produce to create healthy, simple dishes.

DAILY MEALS

A traditional Danish breakfast, or *Morgenmad*, involves bread and butter, cheese, possibly cold meats and coffee. Porridge and beer-and-bread porridge *(Øllebrød)* are also very occasionally eaten. Of course, many people also eat cereal. Coffee is generally drunk rather than tea. In a hotel, the sheer scope of choice can be overwhelming, especially if faced with plates and plates of small Danish pastries *(wienerbrød)*.

Lunch, or *Frokost*, can vary, but most people have an open sandwich or *smørrebrød*. This is traditionally a piece of dark rye bread with a topping. These can be quite complicated: *Dyrlægens natmad* ('Veterinarian's midnight snack'), for example, consists of liver paté *(leverpostej)*, topped with corned beef *(salt kød)* and a slice of meat aspic *(sky)*, plus raw onion rings and cress.

Other traditional sandwich toppings include smoked eel, scrambled egg and radishes; chopped liver paté with bacon and sauteed mushrooms; thin slices of roast pork *(ribbensteg)* with red sweet-and-sour cabbage; *gravadlax* (slices of smoked or cured salmon on white bread with shrimp, lemon and fresh dill); and, perhaps most complex of all, *Stjerneskud* ('Shooting Star'), which consists of two pieces of fish (one steamed, one fried and battered) on a piece of buttered white bread, piled high with shrimp, mayonnaise, red caviar and a slice of lemon.

A traditional alternative to *smørrebrød*, is to eat from a *Dansk Kold Bord*, or Danish Cold Table. Some restaurants offer these, though it is very typical at home on festive occasions. The cold table is like a buffet, with a cold first course, usually some sort of marinated herring *(marinerede sild)*, which might be pickled or served up in a red or white vinegar dressing. Sour cream sauces are also popular. On extra-festive occasions, the herring might be prepared with other ingredients, such as potato, onions and capers topped with a dill sour cream/mayonnaise sauce. Herring is usually served with ice-cold *snaps*, which, according to the Danes, helps it to swim down to the stomach. The high level of alcohol also helps aid digestion.

The second course will be cold meats and salads, followed by a warm dish *(see box right)*, usually on a piece of rye bread, followed by cheese and biscuits.

Supper is called *Middag* because it used to be eaten in the middle of the day. It is eaten at home and most

Danes make an effort to gather the family around a hot meal every evening. Meat is usually served, often with traditional gravy and potato dishes, although international foods, such as pasta, pizza and American-influenced foods are also popular.

Above from far left: chefs at work; Danes love their berries; a feast for the eyes and the tastebuds.

Traditional Dishes

Æbleflæsk	Pork slices with an apple, onion and bacon compote.
Æggekage	'Egg cake': a substantial omelette-like dish, sometimes made with flour so it rises slightly.
Biksemad	Beef hash served with a fried egg and ketchup.
Blodpølse	Black pudding, made from pig's blood.
Brændende Kærlighed	Called 'Burning Love', this is mashed potato with fried onion and pieces of bacon *(pictured below)*.
Finker	Sweetmeat similar to haggis.
Flæskesteg	Roast pork with crackling *(svær)*.
Frikadeller	Meatballs, Denmark's 'national' dish.
Millionbøf	Tiny pieces of beef in gravy, poured over mashed potato. The name means 'million steak'.
Øllebrød	Porridge made of rye bread, sugar and beer.
Stegte sild i eddike	Fried herring in vinegar.

EATING AT HOME

Food plays an important part both in the Danish psyche, as it brings people together, and in the concept of *'hygge'*, a term hard to translate but meaning something along the lines of 'cosiness, warmth and comfort with good food, drink and company' although it can mean different things to different people. Eating together is an important social event, whether it is a daily family affair or a dinner with non-family guests.

As in most places, there are traditional times of year that the family comes together if it can. In Denmark, a Christmas lunch *(Julefrokost)* and an

Pølsevogn
The *pølsevogn* (sausage wagon) is a fast-food institution. Hotdogs, including the infamous long red sausages *røde pølser*, are served with bread, mustard, ketchup and remoulade, and washed down with chocolate milk.

Below: tasty starter.

Easter lunch *(Påskefrokost)* are traditional. The Christmas table or *Julebordet* is organized like a *Kold Bord*, and, in addition to everyday *smørrebrød* toppings, there will be special Christmas dishes such as *æbleflæsk* (pork slices served with an apple, onion and bacon compote), *flæskesteg* (roast pork with crackling) and *Julesylte*, a pork paté served with pickled beetroot and mustard.

Other traditional foods include goose (though many people now prefer duck), eaten on 24 December with boiled potatoes, pickled red cabbage, tiny caramelised potatoes and gravy and, for pudding, *Ris à l'amande*, a rice pudding served with whipped cream, chopped almonds and cherry sauce. Traditionally, everyone eats until someone finds the whole almond hidden in the pudding. This dish was served first as, in the past, it was used to fill everyone up, so that a small amount of meat would go around (rather like English Yorkshire pudding, which is now served alongside the meat but used to be served first). The meal is usually washed down with beer or *snaps*.

EATING IN RESTAURANTS

Eating out is not a typically Danish occupation, although it is becoming increasingly popular, especially in cities and among the young and those with a disposable income.

In Copenhagen, there are over 2,000 restaurants and cafés, which will usually provide a good meal. There are

also those that will provide something extraordinary: 10 Copenhagen restaurants were awarded 11 Michelin stars in 2011. There was general surprise that the New Nordic restaurant **Noma** did not win a third star in spite of topping the San Pellegrino World's 50 Best Restaurants list.

Copenhagen's cafés are usually open from the morning until late at night and most serve alcohol and will provide food throughout the day and into the evening. Some turn into clubs with music and dancing at night.

Restaurants are usually a bit more formal and the kitchen will close a couple of hours before the last people are expected to leave. If you want to eat late, always ring to find out when the kitchen closes. Restaurants that serve both lunch and supper often stop serving in the late afternoon, so don't be surprised if lunch is not available after about 2pm. For smart restaurants, it is always advisable to book ahead.

WHERE TO BUY FOOD

If you want to buy food yourself, Copenhagen has some excellent food stores. Dubbed a 'gourmet street', Vesterbro's **Værnedamsvej** is a wonderful place to find delicatessens, a high-quality butcher, greengrocer, and wine, cheese and chocolate shops. If you don't get that far, all the department stores are generally worth a visit for their upmarket grocers.

For organic bread, patisserie, wine, chocolate and oil check out one of the many **Emmerys** stores (central out-

lets include Østerbrogade 51; Vesterbrogade 34; Store Strandstraede 21; www.emerys.dk). The new wave of organic delicatessens includes the renowned **Meyers Deli** (Kongens Nytorv 13; Gammel Kongevej 107; Godthåbsvej 10; www.meyersdeli.dk), which also has a dedicated bakery (Store Kongensgade 46). Those with a sweet tooth should head for one of the **Lagkagehuset** (Frederiksberggade 21; Vesterbrogade 4a; Frederiksborggade 6) patisseries to sample Danish cakes and pastries. A growing number of microbreweries offer thirsty travellers pilsner-type beers, from Tivoli's own **Færgekroen Bryghus** (Vesterbrogade 3) to the prize-winning Nørrebro Bryghus (Ryesgade 3; www.noerrebro bryghus.dk).

Eco-Labelling

The Danish mark of inspection for organic products is a red 'Ø' symbol. This indicates that the product has been inspected by the Danish authorities and must meet stringent quality and production regulations. A product can only be marketed as organic if 95 percent of its ingredients are certified by the 'Ø' symbol. The same conditions apply to products bearing the 'Euro-leaf' logo, the EU's official organic label used throughout Europe. The EU flower symbol and the Nordic Council of Ministers' stylised swan symbol are common eco-labels, used on non-food products that do not contain any toxic ingredients and that have been manufactured with the least possible impact to the environment.

Above from far left: Danish blue cheese; Danish pastries; cafés usually open from morning until late at night.

Organic Commitment
Danes are committed to eco-friendly living, and are currently the biggest consumers of organic food in the world. In spite of the global recession, sales of organic products continue to rise, with every Dane spending about €139 per year on organic food. 75 per cent of all food eaten in Copenhagen's public institutions is organic. Although this is a world record, the city is not content to rest on its laurels: it aims to increase organic consumption to 90 per cent by 2015.

SHOPPING

Copenhagen is an appealing, if not wildly cheap, place to shop, especially for Danish designer goods, particularly furniture, household items and clothing. Whether you buy or not, it's a great place for window-shopping.

THE SHOPPING MAP

With plenty of cafés and street entertainment, and over a kilometre of pedestrianised streets, Strøget makes for a stress-free shopping experience. The quality of the goods in its mainstream shops improves as you head up the street from Rådhuspladsen, reaching a rather smart conclusion up by Kongens Nytorv, with designer boutiques and furriers such as Gucci and Burberry, and Danish designers Sand and Birger Christensen.

Vimmelskaftet, Amagertorv and Østergade are home to some of Denmark's most famous names. Here you'll find Lego's flagship emporium; the 120-year-old department store Illums; its sister store, Illums Bolighus, which will fulfil all your designer desires for household gadgets and wonderful Danish furniture and lighting; Royal Copenhagen, with its world-famous china (and the opportunity to paint your own, *see p.36*); Georg Jensen, the father of simply designed silver jewellery (at a price); and Hay House, an important stop for minimalist furniture and colourful rugs.

Magasin du Nord, an elegant department store located on Kongens Nytorv, will take care of your sartorial needs. Up the road, Danish audio wizards Bang & Olufsen have their main store.

Do not be afraid to wander off Strøget into the streets adjoining it, as it is here that you will find lots of independently owned, quirky little shops. Tucked off the main thoroughfare are gems such as Stilleben at Niels Hemmingsensgade 3, which sells unusual homeware and hand-made ceramics; or Norse Store at Pilestræde 41, a must for fashion-conscious chaps.

Farvergade, Kompagnistræde and Laederstræde run parallel to Strøget in one uninterrupted pedestrian street, lined with shops dealing in oriental rugs, antique furniture, silverware, china and curios. The prices aren't exactly low, but on a good day it's possible to find a fair deal. These streets are more popular than Strøget among Copenhageners and the cafés are always full of people. On Laederstræde, check out Grønlykke (No. 3) for funky and kitsch home furnishings. Hidden away in a basement next door at No. 5 is Wettergren & Wettergren, whose owners update vintage clothing and accessories. For girlie presents, such as pastel porcelain and flowery cushions, try Liebe at No. 23 Kompagnistræde,

The Latin Quarter, close to the university, is home to several book shops (*boghandel*) and second-hand clothing and record shops. There is also a

Tax-Free Shopping
If you make large purchases in tax-free stores, you will be able to reclaim your tax *(see p.101)* – a welcome bonus in a city that isn't the cheapest, but where home quality is usually very good.

summer flea market on Gammel Strand (Sat–Sun 8am–2pm) and flower stalls round the back of Magasin du Nord. For a very exotic floral experience (though astonishingly they charge to let you in), have a look in the window of designer florist Tage Andersen at Ny Adelgade 12.

Kronprinsensgade, north of Strøget, contains many of Denmark's designer clothes shops, like the exclusive Bruuns Bazaar at No. 9.

Away from the Centre
Elsewhere, there are plenty of opportunities to seek out independent little shops. Out in Nørrebro, for example, around Sankt Hans Torv, you will find antique and bric-a-brac shops on Ravensborggade, vintage clothing on Blågardsgade and young, eclectic clothes shops run by aspiring designers in streets such as Elmegade – try design collective Fünf at No. 2, urban fashionistas Goggle at No. 3 or Elmebørn at No. 21 for cute kids' clothing.

Nansensgade near the reservoirs is an up-and-coming area, with a smattering of interesting shops and cafés.

Better still is trendy Vesterbro: Istedgade boasts various boutiques run by young artists and designers, some still experimenting with their styles. Long-standing favourites include Donn Ya Doll at No. 55, with a mouthwatering choice of 30 clothes designers; Asfalt at No. 83, selling unique outfits made from recycled fabric; and Kyoto at No. 95, with a cool selection of understated Scandinavian fashion. In the same district, Designer Zoo (Vesterbrogade 137)

showcases the creations of eight Danish designers, who work on the premises in glass, ceramics, wool and gold.

If you are after authentic antiques, Bredgade near the Amalienborg is full of shops and auction houses.

DANISH HOUSEHOLD DESIGN

Danish furniture ranks among the world's best. Here you'll see items credited to the designer rather than to the factory. Furniture is a national pride and most good pieces will have a black circular 'Danish Furniture-Makers' sticker attached. Lamps are also lovingly designed, as are household textiles and hand-woven rugs.

If you want your shops under one roof, the best places are Illums Bolighus, Casa (Store Regnegade 2; www.casagroup. com) or, north of Osterbrø, the designer furniture store, Paustian (Kalkbrænderiløbskaj 2; www.paustian.dk).

ENTERTAINMENT

There is lots to do in the evenings in Copenhagen, above and beyond eating out. These pages will get you started, with general information about the main concert venues and nightlife hotspots: for individual bar and club listings, see the Nightlife section on p122.

Above: Rust has live acts and plenty to drink.

Royal Danish Playhouse
The Royal Danish Playhouse is one of the newest addition to the Copenhagen cultural and architectural scene. On the waterfront near Nyhavn, it provides a visual, modern balance to the opera house a little further up the Sound opposite the Amalienborg. Almost half the building is constructed in the water, partly on new fill and partly on detached piles.

TIVOLI

An evening visit to **Tivoli** *(see p.75)* is a must, even if it is just for a wander to take in the lights, fireworks and the atmosphere. If you wish to be a little more focussed, the open-air stage has free evening concerts on Fridays. There is also an impressive concert hall *(see below)*, with a shark tank in the foyer.

CONCERT HALLS

The **Tivoli Concert Hall** (tel: 33 15 10 12) is one of the largest classical venues for ballet, opera and classical music in Copenhagen; it also puts on rock concerts and is a major venue during the jazz festival in July. You will need to book in advance.

The Danish Symphony Orchestra were treated to a fabulous new home in 2009: the **DR Koncerthuset** (Emil Holms Kanal 20; customer service tel: 35 20 62 62, ticket sales tel: 70 26 32 67; www.dr.dk/koncerthuset) on Amager, designed by Frenchman Jean Nouvel, is a jaw-dropping piece of architectue and the most expensive concert hall ever built. Its spaces are used for pop, rock and jazz as well as classical concerts.

THEATRE, OPERA AND DANCE

There are several places on offer – some more dependent on an understanding of Danish than others. The **Opera House** (Operaen; Ekvipagemestervej 10, Holmen; tel: 33 69 69 69; *see p.87*) is a wonderful evening out offering both traditional and modern opera and ballet in a startling building. The auditorium is very comfortable with excellent visibility and acoustics. Ticket prices vary but start from around 95dkk for a concert or an opera. Top opera tickets rarely rise beyond 895dkk.

Its sister venue the **Royal Theatre** (Det Kongelige Teater; tel: 33 69 69 69; www.kglteater.dk) puts on some concerts and ballets, but its functions have mostly been superseded by the Opera House and the **Royal Danish Playhouse** (Skuespilhuset; Kvæsthusbroen; tel: 33 69 69 33; www.kglteater.dk), which opened in 2008 on the waterfront near Nyhavn. It has two big stages – the main stage with 650 seats and Portscenen with 200 seats – together with a studio stage, restaurant, café and a large public square in front of the building with harbour views. For some performances the north wall can

be opened up on to the quayside.

The **New Theatre** (Det Ny Teater; Gammel Kongevej 29; 33 25 60 05; www.detnyteater.dk) just off Vesterbrogade does a roaring trade in big musicals such as West Side Story, My Fair Lady, Phantom of the Opera, The Producers and Chicago.

JAZZ CLUBS AND DINNER-DANCES

Copenhagen has a bit of a reputation for jazz, with a renowned 10-day international festival held at the beginning of July. The **Copenhagen Jazz House** (the city's premier jazz spot) and **Mojo's** (a smaller, more intimate venue) should tide you over until festival time.

If you fancy an all-in-one bit of entertainment, try out **Wallmans Saloner** (Cirkusbygningen, Jernbanegade 8; tel: 33 16 37 00; www. wallmans.dk; Thur–Sat from 6.30pm; show 7pm–11.15pm, dancing to 1am; prices around 400dkk-800dk), where your evening takes in a meal and stage entertainment (glamorous dancers, singers and acrobats), followed by a night of dancing.

BARS, CLUBS AND DISCOS

Copenhagen has plenty of cool drinking places, from rustic bistros to chic modern bars to cosy cellar pubs. Danes take pride in their lager-style beers, and there are several excellent brew-pubs, such as **Nørrebro**

Bryghus, where you can sample beer made on the premises. Copenhageners love a cocktail – you'll find plenty of shaking and stirring going on around town.

There are no shortage of places to dance the night away, including many late-opening cafés and bars. **Vega**, in Vesterbro, is one of the oldest and biggest nightclubs. Vesterbro is also where you'll find the former butchers' district Kødbyen, which has seen an incredible reinvention over the past few years and is now one of the city's hottest areas for wining, dining and partying. New places are still opening there: be sure to check it out. The most exciting nightlife venues seem to spring up in the city's edgier areas - Nørrebro also has its share of up-and-coming bars, and clubs such as **Rust**, which offers live bands and international DJs.

Of course, the best parties are the ones that you stumble upon accidentally – ask the locals.

Listings

For listings of what is going on in Copenhagen, including cinema listings (most films are shown in their original version with subtitles) check out The Copenhagen Post (www.cphpost. dk), the English-language weekly newspaper. The tourist board website, www.visitcopenhagen. com also has a diary of events.

Below: dancing is fun at Rust.

HISTORY: KEY DATES

An expanding and contracting economic and political power, Denmark has, in its time, ruled over much of Europe and Scandinavia. It is now an independent-minded member of the EU.

VIKING PERIOD

*c.*AD700–1000	The Vikings colonize Britain, Normandy and much of southern Sweden, and also reach Greenland, Canada, North Africa, Russia and Constantinople.
960	Harald Bluetooth converts to Christianity.

MIDDLE AGES

Above: Viking ship; Bishop Absalon.

1157	Valdemar I accedes to the throne and unifies Denmark after a century of unrest.
*c.*1160	Bishop Absalon builds the first castle on Slotsholmen.
1254	Købmandshavn (Copenhagen) receives a charter. The German Hanseatic League recognises its important role in Baltic trade.
1282	Danish nobles force the unpopular king Erik V to sign the Great Charter at Nyborg, limiting his authority.
1340	Accession of Valdemar Atterdag (1340–75) who reinforces royal power and expands its territories.
1397	Margrethe I (1375–1412) sets up the Kalmar Union, an alliance with Norway and Sweden, in which Denmark rules all three.
1417	Margrethe's grandnephew, Erik VII, builds Kronborg Castle at Helsingør, a fortress and 'toll booth' to collect money from ships passing through the Sound.
1425–79	Copenhagen flourishes and grows. In 1443, it becomes Denmark's capital and in 1479, Copenhagen University is founded.

Old Ruins
The foundations of Slotsholmen Castle are considered the most important ruins in the capital today. You can see them now beneath Christiansborg Palace in the centre of Copenhagen.

RENAISSANCE

1523–34	The Kalmar Union ends with Gustav Vasa's coronation as King of Sweden. Norway remains part of Denmark until 1814.
1536	The Reformation: Denmark becomes a Protestant country.
1588–1648	Copenhagen booms and the city expands in the 60-year reign of Christian IV but Denmark's entry (1525–29) into the Thirty

Years' War (1618–48) against the Holy Roman Empire is a costly disaster. Further fighting (1643–45) against Swedish forces sees heavy Danish territorial losses.

Above from far left: Copenhagen on the map; the Øresund bridge links Denmark to Sweden.

1658–59 Denmark loses another war with Sweden, ceding a third of its territories, including control over the profitable Sound.

1665 Frederik III establishes an hereditary absolute monarchy.

18TH AND 19TH CENTURIES

1711–12 Plague claims a third of Copenhagen's population.

1728 Major fires gut much of the city leading to reconstruction.

1754 The Royal Danish Academy of Art is founded, inspiring a 'Golden Age' (1800–50) of the arts.

1788 Serfdom is abolished.

1801–14 Neutral Copenhagen is bombarded by the English Navy to prevent her from doing business with France. Britain attacks again in 1807. Denmark sides with France and is bankrupt by 1813. Denmark loses Norway to Sweden in the Treaty of Kiel.

1848–9 Frederik VII abolishes absolute monarchy.

1864 After war with Prussia and Austria, Denmark cedes her territories of Schleswig and Holstein to Germany.

20TH AND 21ST CENTURIES

1914–18 Denmark remains neutral during the First World War.

1929–40 Welfare state is set up under a left-wing coalition dominated by the Social Democrats. Economic depression in the 1930s.

1940–45 Neutral Denmark is invaded by Germany in 1940. It joins the Allies in 1943 and the Resistance takes most of the Jewish population to safety in Sweden. Britain liberates Denmark in 1945.

1968–71 Christiania is founded after student unrest.

1972 Margrethe II becomes queen.

1973 Denmark joins the EEC (EU).

1989 Denmark is the first country to recognise same-sex marriages.

2000 Denmark votes against the euro. The Øresund Bridge, a rail and road link with Sweden, opens.

2001 Right-wing coalition unexpectedly takes power.

2006 *Jyllands-Posten* causes offence to the Muslim world by publishing 12 cartoons depicting the Prophet Muhammed.

2011 Helle Thorning-Schmidt, Denmark's first female prime minister, leads a centre-left coalition into power.

CoBrA
A group of artists set up the abstract movement CoBrA (Copenhagen-Brussels-Amsterdam), painting in an expressionistic, avant-garde style with emphasis on brushwork and colour. Its leading exponent was painter Asger Jorn (1914–73); others included Pierre Alechinsky and Karel Appel.

WALKS AND TOURS

VESTERBRO

This walk takes you from Central Station through Vesterbro, Copenhagen's former red-light district. Vesterbro retains its seamier edges, but is also one of the most vibrant parts of the city: Istedgade is full of one-off boutiques, and buzzing cafés, bars and restaurants pack the old butchers' quarter Kødbyen.

Vesterbro

Vesterbro literally means 'West Bridge'; the west bridge crossed the city moat (the remains of which are the reservoirs that run from Vesterbro up to Østerbro, 'East Bridge') to the West Door or 'Vesterport' into the city.

DISTANCE 5km (3 miles)

TIME A half/full day

START Hovedbanegården

END Bakkehuset

POINTS TO NOTE

This is quite a lengthy walk. If you want to speed things up and possibly combine with all or part of the Frederiksberg Walk *(see p.67)*, after Værnedamsvej, take a 6A bus down Vesterbro to Pile Allé (turn left for Carlsberg) or on to the zoo.

Until the mid-19th century, Vesterbrogade, Vesterbro's main street, was the paved and busy road that led to Copenhagen's west gate, or 'Vesterport', through a country area mainly put to pasture with a few industrial buildings and timber yards. Until 1853, building outside the city walls was not allowed except with express permission. However, with the rise of industrialisation, dreadful sanitation, increased pressure on living space within the city walls and a cholera outbreak in June 1853, which killed

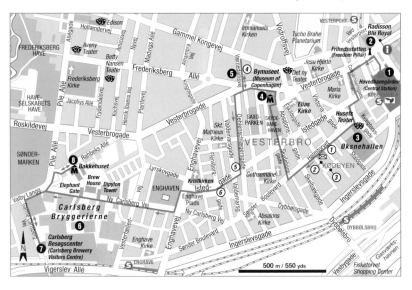

around 4,500 people, this prohibition was lifted. In 1856, the city ramparts and gates were pulled down, and there was no longer a barrier between the city and the land beyond. Building began in earnest in all the 'bro' ('bridge') districts beyond the city.

Vesterbro was never an expensive area and when the red-light district in Pisserenden was cleared out in the early 1900s, many of its workers came to Vesterbro. There is still a red-light district here, but it is contained in a few streets, and the area is better represented by the resident immigrant population and the young artists and designers who also favour the area.

In the past, living conditions here have been poor; there are still some problems but gentrification has begun to set in and restoration and improvements have been made. Nonetheless, if you are wondering where the grittier side of life is to be found in Copenhagen, you will find some of it here.

OUTSIDE THE STATION

Start outside **Hovedbanegården ❶**, designed in 1911 by the prolific railway architect Heinrich Wenck, who drafted plans for 150 of Denmark's stations. The country's first railway line (built in 1847–8) ran from here to Roskilde *(see p.88)*. Look left, and in the middle of the road you will see an obelisk, the **Freedom Pillar** (Frihedstøtten).

The Freedom Pillar

Unveiled in 1797, when it stood outside the city walls, the Freedom Pillar commemorates the end of adscription in 1788, which meant that peasants could leave the estate where they were born and choose to live and work elsewhere. Before this, they were legally tied to their feudal lord and could be hunted down, brought back and punished severely if they tried to leave. The four figures represent Loyalty, Civic Virtue, Cultivating the Soil and Valour.

Radisson Blu Royal Hotel

The tower block on the corner of Vesterbrogade and Hammerichsgade is the **Radisson Blu Royal Hotel ❷**, an icon in the history of architecture erected in 1960 by Arne Jacobsen (1902–71), the architect/designer credited with almost single-handedly creating the world's concept of practical but stylish and elegant Danish design. **Room 606** is the only one that retains Jacobsen's original design; if it's not booked and you ask nicely at reception, you might be able to see it. The 20th-floor restaurant **Alberto K** provides wonderful evening meals and panoramic views.

INTO VESTERBRO

Turn left down Vesterbrogade, and left again onto Colbjørnsensgade. You are now in the red-light area. A recent influx of young families and hip bars and restaurants has diluted this notorious district, although you'll still see a few disreputable clubs and interesting window displays. Turn right into Istedgade and left down Helgoslandgade into Halmtorvet, a former haymarket

Above from far left: the sweeping view from the Alberto K restaurant; trendy Vesterbro bar; bull sculpture in Kødbyen.

Swans and Eggs
Arne Jacobsen was involved in every aspect of the Radisson Blu Royal Hotel's design, even down to the door handles and cutlery. In the lobby you will see the famous 'Egg' and 'Swan' chairs, designed especially for this hotel more than 50 years ago.

Independent Shops and Cafés

Vesterbro is popular with young designers and you will come across some quirky, unusual shopping as you do this walk, including some good second-hand stores.

and now home to several cafés. Opposite is **Øksnehallen ❸** (Halmtorvet 11; tel: 33 29 81 19; charge for exhibitions), an old cattle market now regenerated into a large and lovely cultural space.

Kødbyen

Stretching several blocks to the west is Kødbyen ('Meat Town'), the former butchers' district, which has reinvented itself as one of the most dynamic areas of Copenhagen. The former cattle pens, slaughterhouses and market halls now contain gallery spaces, small, creative companies, and the city's coolest bars, cafés and clubs. Stop here for lunch at one of the many fabulous restaurants, including the all-organic **Bio Mio**, see ⑪①, pizza-makers **Mother**, see ⑪②, or **Kødbyens Fiskebar**, see ⑪③; or return after sundown to sample the area's lively nightlife.

Continue down Halmtorvet and turn right six streets down into **Skydebanegade**. Walk past the yellow townhouses and cross the main road. Go through the gate in the imposing brick wall opposite, which leads into **Skydebanehaven**, a park that once belonged to the Royal Shooting Club (now the

---

Food and Drink 🍴

① BIO MIO
Halmtorvet 19; tel: 33 31 20 00; http://biomio.dk; daily noon–9.30pm; €
Organic, self-service canteen, whose super-fresh dishes are ordered directly with the chef then consumed at communal tables.

② MOTHER
Høkerboderne 9–15; tel: 22 27 58 98; Sun–Wed 11am–11pm, Thu–Sat 11am–1am; €
Opened in 2010, this quickly became one of the city's favourite pizza places thanks to its cosy atmosphere and small, select menu of sourdough creations.

③ KØDBYENS FISKEBAR
Høkerboderne 9-15; tel: 22 27 58 98; Sun–Wed 11am–11pm, Thu–Sat 11am–1am; €
This fashionable bistro, with its chic urban interior and mesmerising jellyfish tank, serves superb poached cockles, Limfjorden oysters and razor clams.

④ LES TROIS COCHONS
Værnedamsvej 10; tel: 33 31 70 55; www.cofoco.dk; Mon–Sat noon–2.30pm, daily 5.30pm–10pm; €
This atmospheric, elegant old butcher's shop delivers both style and good food (in the form of a three-course set menu) at a very good price.

⑤ BANG AND JENSEN
Istedgade 130; tel: 33 25 53 18; Mon–Fri 8am–2am, Sat 10am–2am, Sun 10am–midnight; €
A former pharmacy, now a cool and very popular café-bar. Particularly good brunches.

⑥ RICCOS
Istedgade 119; tel: 31 21 04 40; daily 9am–10pm; €
Tiny coffee house that does excellent coffee.

City Museum), one of the first buildings in Vesterbro.

Walk through the kids' play area and follow the path to the exit, turning left onto Absalonsgade. Take a left onto Vesterbrogade; the **Museum of Copenhagen** (Kobenhavns ByMuseet) is located on your left, housed in the club's stately mansion house which dates back to the early 18th century.

The Museum of Copenhagen

The **Museum of Copenhagen** ❹ (Vesterbrogade 59; tel: 33 21 07 72; 10am–5pm daily; charge, under-17s free, Fri free) takes you from Copenhagen's early days as a small fishing village to modern times, using some atmospheric reconstructions as well as fascinating objects from the collection. The museum has been closely involved in the city-wide excavation works for the new metro system which have revealed some interesting finds.

Værnedamsvej

Back on Vesterbrogade, turn left and continue to the junction with Frederiksberg Allé. Then, turn right up **Værnedamsvej** ❺, famous for its gourmet shopping and a good place for lunch or early supper; try **Les Trois Cochons**, see ⑪④. Once you've finished exploring this tasty little street, return to Vesterbrogade and then cross the road into Oehlenschlægersgade where you will find, on the corner with Kaalundsgade, an extraordinary mosaic-covered building, reminiscent of Gaudi's work in Barcelona – all lovingly put together by the late Nigerian-born artist Manuel Tafat.

The Carlsberg Brewery

Continue to the end of the street and turn right along Istegade. If you want an afternoon coffee, there are several good cafés along here, notably **Bang and Jensen**, see ⑪⑤, and tiny **Riccos**, see ⑪⑥, as well as some interesting independent shops. After passing four streets, turn left onto Enghavevej. Keep going and turn right at a large crossroads onto Ny Carlsberg Vej, where you are heading for the **Carlsberg Brewery** ❻ (Carlsberg Bryggerierne).

You can see an archway from the end of the road. As you get there, look to

Carlsberg Beer

The Carlsberg brewery was set up by ale-brewer Jacob Christian Jacobsen (1811–87) in 1847, the year that he produced his first commercial beer using the new German lagering process. He named the brewery after his five-year old son Carl (1842–1914); 'berg' refers to the hill on which it was built. Carl built a second brewery close by in 1882 and took the swastika, an ancient sacred symbol found in a number of civilizations including Greece and Rome, as the new Carlsberg trademark. Both father and son espoused perfection, Jacobsen *père* even citing it in his will, 'In working the brewery it should be a constant purpose, regardless of immediate gain, to develop the art of making beer to the greatest possible degree of perfection'.

your left to see the tall **winding chimney** decorated with lotus flowers (hard to see from a distance) and gargoyles (copied from Notre-Dame in Paris). Carlsberg want to prove that an industrial chimney could be beautiful so commissioned one of Copenhagen's most celebrated architects, Vilhelm Dahlerup, to design this one in 1900.

The first archway, called the **Dipylon Gate**, was built in 1892 and originally housed two malting floors; malt was loaded in and out of carriages through tubes in the gate's ceiling. The figure group on the roof, by sculptor Stephen Sinding, is called *The Bell Strikers*. The mosaics on the other side of the gate show Carl Jacobsen, his wife Ottilia and son and heir Alf (who died in 1890); Vilhelm Dahlerup and master builder S.P. Beckmann; and four figures representing the brewery's employees.

Go through and you will see another archway held up by the four, famous lifesize **Carlsberg elephants**. They were partly inspired by the elephants holding up the organ in Our Saviour's Church (Vor Frelsers Kirke, *see p.84*) and partly by Bernini's obelisk-carrying elephant in Piazza Minerva in Rome. Note the copper busts of Carl and Ottilia Jacobsen looking down from a gallery at the top of the gate.

The Renaissance-style building on the right of the gate is the **Brew**

Above: the famous elephants mark the entrance to the old brewery.

Getting Home
If you don't want to walk all the way home, head down Rahbeks Allé away from Pile Allé, to Vesterbrogade, where you can pick up the 6A bus back into town.

Right: the Carlsberg Visitor Centre contains the world's largest collection of beer bottles – 20,000 and counting!

House, with a balcony modelled on those in the Palazzo Bavilaque in Verona. On the roof is a large copper sculpture representing *Thor's Battle Against the Giants*.

Walk under the 'Elephant Gate' to the end, passing, on your left, the former Carlsberg Museum, now used as a restaurant. Turn left onto Valby Langgade and then take the first left into Gamle Carlsberg Vej, where about half way down on the left you will find the **Carlsberg Visitor Centre**.

The Carlsberg Visitor Centre

The **Carlsberg Visitor Centre** ❼ (Carlsberg Besøgscenter; Gamle Carlsberg Vej 11; tel: 33 27 12 82; www.visitcarlsberg.dk; Tue–Sun 10am–5pm; charge) is in listed buildings that belonged to the first brewery; they date from 1867 when they were rebuilt following a fire. The exhibition offers interesting insight into brewing past and present, using light, sound, smells and interactive media. You can also view a collection of Carlsberg label and bottle designs, see the dray horses in their stables and, of course, sample (for free) a beer (or soft drink) in an airy bar, dominated by great copper brewing kettles.

If you have time to visit the **Bakkehuset**, the oldest building in the area, dating from the 1650s when it was an inn on the road to Copenhagen, retrace your steps to the top of Ny Carlsberg Vej and continue down Pile Allé. Take the second right and the museum is on the right-hand side.

Bakkehuset

From 1787, the **Bakkehuset** ❽ (Rahbeks Allé 23, tel: 33 31 43 62; www.bakkehusmuseet.dk; Tue–Sun 11am–4pm; charge), was home to Kamma and Knud Lyne Rahbek, literary personalities of the 19th-century Golden Age *(see p.59)*. It is now a cultural museum, furnished in a rather sparse romantic style. The poets Johannes Ewald (1743–81) and Adam Oehlenschläger (1779–1850, *see box*), are featured heavily (Oehlenschläger was the Rahbeks' son-in-law) and there is also memorabilia relating to Hans Christian Andersen (1805–75, *see p.56*), who came here often in his youth.

Above from far left: an old cart used to transport beer out of the brewery; Carlsberg Pilsner or Carlsberg Lager is the beer most people expect when ordering a Carlsberg.

Nordic Romance

Born in Vesterbro, Adam Oehlenschläger (1779–1850) was the pioneer of Romantic poetry and drama in Denmark. He was first inspired in 1802 after a 16-hour conversation with the Danish philosopher Henrik Steffens, who was causing a sensation lecturing on the hitherto unknown 'modern' German poets Goethe and Schiller. By the age of 26, Oehlenschläger was universally recognised as Denmark's leading poet. He is also the author of Denmark's national anthem, 'Der er et Yndigt Land' ('There is a Lovely Country').

THE OLD INNER CITY

This circular walk takes you through the oldest part of Copenhagen and encompasses Strøget, Copenhagen's long 'walking street', Gammel Strand (Old Beach) and the University or Latin Quarter. It is now a very lively area full of shops, bars and restaurants.

DISTANCE 3.5km (2 miles)
TIME A half/full day
START/END Rådhuspladsen
POINTS TO NOTE

This walk takes quite a while if you visit everything. However, if you want to combine part of it with other walks, from Højbro Plads you can visit Slotsholmen *(see p.76)* or continue down Strøget to Kongens Nytorv and Nyhavn *(see pp.43–6)*.

Above from top:
taking a leisurely walk on Strøget;
the Caritas Fountain.

Look Up
Oddly enough, it can be easy to miss the architecture on Strøget, so much is going on at eye-level. But don't forget to look up to see the variety of styles and decorations in this ancient, if relatively newly built, quarter.

With the exception of Slotsholmen *(see p.76)*, this is the oldest part of Copenhagen. Predominantly built in wood, the old city was a martyr to fire and almost completely demolished in 1728 and 1795. The first fire destroyed nearly 50 per cent of the medieval city and made 20 per cent of the population homeless; the second pretty much finished off the job. So, although the area has been inhabited for over 700 years, there are very few buildings that remain from before the 18th century.

Start at Rådhuspladsen *(see p.74)*, which was built in the 19th century just inside the old city walls (now demolished) and walk down Frederiksberggade, one of the five streets that make up **Strøget** (literally 'stripe'

and pronounced 'stroll'), the world's longest pedestrianised street, which reaches all the way to royal Kongens Nytorv *(see p.43)* by the harbour.

This western end of Strøget is the least sophisticated part, characterised by fast-food joints and cheap fashion stores, in contrast with the middle and final stretches, where you will find Danish design and top fashion brands.

GAMMELTORV

Follow the cobbles to the first large open area that you come to. This is the site of Havn, Copenhagen's oldest village. **Gammeltorv ❶** (Old Square), on your left, is the city's oldest meeting place where, in the Middle Ages, everything took place; a little like Rådhuspladsen today.

Gammeltorv suffered in both fires and the town hall that had stood facing inwards on what is now the intersection with **Nytorv ❷** (New Square), was burnt down on both occasions. Rebuilt in the same place after 1728, after the second fire it was rebuilt on Nytorv *(see opposite)*, in the hope that the space created would act as a windbreak in the event of another fire. You can see its old outline in pale stone where the fruit-and-vegetable market usually stands.

On your left, you will see the **Caritas Fountain** (Springvandet). This is Copenhagen's oldest external water supply and is linked by pipes to a water source 6km (4 miles) away. It was a gift to the city in 1608 from Christian IV: the pregnant, lactating woman with her two children represents *Caritas* (Charity). The fountain becomes extra glitzy on important royal birthdays, when it is filled with golden apples.

The curved facade of **Stellings Hus**, designed by Arne Jacobsen (who also designed the Radisson Blu Royal Hotel *(see p.27)*, stands nearby on the corner of Skindergade.

NYTORV

On your right is where the gallows and whipping post used to stand on Nytorv. Branding and whipping took place until the late 1780s. The outline of the paler stones on Nytorv shows the position of the whipping post.

On the right-hand side, on the former site of the Royal Orphanage, which burnt down in the fire of 1728, you will find the classical porticoed grandeur of the **Domhuset**, the third town hall. This was built by the architect C.F. Hansen between 1805–15 (with a delay in 1807 when the British bombarded the city); Hansen was also responsible for rebuilding the cathedral, Church of Our Lady *(see p.42)*. The Domhuset was the town hall until 1905 when, owing to space issues, a new one was built on Rådhuspladsen (Town Hall Square). It is still used as Copenhagen's main Law Court (hence the large inscription above the ionic columns, "By law shall the land

Above from far left: statue on Kobmagergade; fashionable Strøget; the old city rooftops.

Gallows on Nytorv
Executions at the gallows on Nytorv were well attended by the locals and, shockingly, for many were a form of entertainment. Between 1720 and 1730 there were 14 executions; sadly, most of them impoverished women driven to killing their newborn babies. The last execution, of two counterfeiters, took place in 1758.

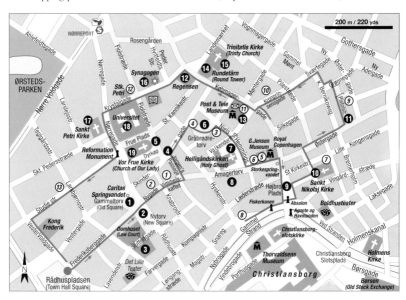

be built") and is the largest in Denmark. On its far side, on **Slutterigade ❸** (Prison Street), you can see the two enclosed bridges that linked the courthouse to the prison.

The Bells Toll

At 8pm on Thursday 20 October, just before the 1728 fire took hold of Helligåndskirken, its carillon bells, which rang out every half hour, played 'Turn your anger, Lord, by mercy'.

Below right: fountain in Gråbrødretorv.

INTO THE LATIN QUARTER

Carry on down Strøget until you reach the crossroads of Knabrostræde and Skoubogade – take a left for chocolate heaven at **PB Chokolade**, see ⑪①, or **La Glace,** see ⑪②. Otherwise, continue until you see a sign for **Jorgen's Passage ❹** on your left, an appealing arcade with some good kids' and home decor shops. Walk through to the end. Opposite is **Fiolstræde ❺** – in the centre of the Latin Quarter around the university – with a few pretty outdoor restaurants and the back of the Church of Our Lady (Vor Frue Kirke). To experience something of the studious atmosphere, visit the excellent antiquarian/second-hand bookshop at 34–36 or grab a coffee at the library-like book café at 10–12.

Gråbrødretorv

Turn right down Skindergade (Hide Street), originally home to furriers and tanners, and walk through to **Gråbrødretorv ❻** (Grey Brothers Square), a delightful square named after the grey-clad monks who lived here from 1238 in Copenhagen's first monastery. The

---

Food and Drink 🍴

① PB CHOKOLADE
Skoubogade 1; tel: 33 93 07 17; €€€
Not cheap but delicious. Specialities include delicacies filled with cream, fruit, nuts, truffle, spices and alcohol.

② LA GLACE
Skoubogade 3–5; tel: 33 14 46 46; www.laglace.dk; Mon–Thur 8.30am–5.30pm, Fri 8.30am–6pm, Sat 9am– 5pm, Sun (Sept–Mar) 10am–5pm (serving stops 30 mins earlier); €€
This traditional cake shop/café dating from 1870 is a Copenhagen institution. They make cakes for the queen so they must be good!

③ PEDER OXE
Gråbrødretorv 11; tel: 33 11 00 77; www.pederoxe.dk; 11.30am–10.30pm; €€
Offers everything from a light lunch, tradtional sandwich or salad bar to full three-course meal. Emphasis on fresh organic produce. Friendly and based in an 18th-century building.

④ SPORVEJEN
Grabrødretorv 17; tel: 33 13 31 01; Mon–Sat 11am–midnight, Sun noon–midnight; €
Cheap and cheerful fare (omelettes, burgers etc) in an old Copenhagen tram. Sit out on the square in summer.

monks were turned out just before the Reformation in 1536, and the monastery became a hospital. Many of the houses here date from after the fire of 1728 and are known as 'fire houses', a gabled, brick-built design that was introduced in the hope that it would be more fire-safe than the medieval timbered buildings that burnt so easily.

The second fire of 1795 destroyed much of the rebuild – the style that followed was plainer and more classical. The square is now filled with restaurants and is a pleasant place to eat out in summer. **Peder Oxe**, see ⑪③, or **Sporvejen**, see ⑪④, are good options if you are already thinking about lunch.

Church of the Holy Ghost

Cross the square and then take a right onto Niels Hemmingsensgade. The church here is the **Church of the Holy Ghost ❼** (Helligåndskirken; Niels Hemmingsensgade 5; tel: 33 37 65 40; www.helligaandskirken.dk; Mon–Fri noon–4pm; Sunday service 10am).

A hospice stood on this site as early as 1296. It was incorporated into the monastery in 1474. Most of the church, including the bells that were given by Christian IV in 1647, was destroyed in 1728. Even the coffins under the floor were destroyed. What survived the fire – the **Helligåndshuset** (now used for markets and exhibitions); **Christian IV's baroque portal**, the main door, made in 1630 and originally intended for the Stock Exchange *(see p.77)*; and **Griffenfeld's Chapel** (the round burial chapel on the north side) – constitute some of the oldest

architectural remains in Copenhagen. The church was reopened in 1732. Admirers of the philosopher Søren Kirkegaard might like to note that it was here that he first saw Régine, the girl to whom he became engaged, but whom he subsequently rejected.

AMAGERTORV

Turn left out of the church back onto Strøget and you are almost immediately on **Amagertorv ❽**, another square punctuating the 1.5km (1-mile) length

Above from far left: street performer; Gråbrødretorv is a delightful café square; colourful Skindergade houses.

Architecture after 1728

The terrible fire of 1728 raged for three days, destroying much of medieval Copenhagen. Surprisingly, when the flames died down, plans to rebuild the city in a more fireproof style were met with widespread opposition. Very few of the streets were widened – people were loath to lose their land to roadways – and although some narrow 'fire houses' were built, much of the construction was done in wood, as it was cheaper than brick.

After a second conflagration in 1795, the construction of houses in brick was enforced, and terraces had to have oblique corners to enable fire engines to get around more easily, thus creating small octagonal squares all over the city. Styles changed and unadorned neoclassical facades, without balconies, became popular.

Modern 17th-Century Design

Formerly the modern town house of a wealthy 17th-century merchant, Amagertorv 6 still sees the rich passing through its portals to buy beautiful porcelain from Royal Copenhagen.

Below right: time for a break.

of Strøget. From here on, the shopping on Strøget becomes infinitely smarter.

Georg Jensen, Royal Copenhagen and Stork Fountain

To your left you will find two great Danish design institutions, the silversmith **Georg Jensen** (Amagertorv 4; tel: 33 11 40 80; Mon–Thur 10am–6pm, Fri 10am–7pm, Sat 10am–5pm; free) and **Royal Copenhagen** (Amagertorv 6; tel: 33 13 71 81; www.royalcopenhagen.com; Mon–Sat 10am–6pm; free), the hand-painted porcelain manufacturer. They are housed side by side in two ornate, rather lovely Renaissance buildings. Georg Jensen's has a small free

museum in the basement.

Next door is **Illums Bolighus**, a furniture design mecca *(see p.18)* and ahead of you, the **Stork Fountain**, Storkespringvandet, erected in 1894 to mark the silver wedding of Crown Prince Frederik (VIII) and his wife, Princess Louise. It's a popular meeting place, and also where newly-qualified Danish midwives come for a celebratory dance!

If you are in need of a drink or a bite to eat, three good places spring to mind: the café at the top of **Illums**, see ⑪⑤, the powder-puff-pink **Royal Café**, see ⑪⑥, or the charming **Restaurant Maven**, see ⑪⑦, a short walk away at the Church of St Nicholas.

HØJBRO PLADS

From here, turn right into **Højbro Plads ❾**, home to a dramatic equestrian statue of Copenhagen's founder,

---

Food and Drink

⑤ ILLUMS BOLIGHUS
Amagertorv 10; tel: 33 14 19 41; Mon–Fri 10am–7pm, Sat 10am–6pm; €
Light, airy, top-floor café with balcony, family area and good coffee.

⑥ THE ROYAL CAFE
Amagertorv 6; tel: 33 12 11 22; www.royalcafe.dk; Mon–Sat 10am–6pm, Sun 11am–5pm; €–€€
Café with courtyard set in a Renaissance building. All dishes are served on Royal Copenhagen porcelain. 'Smushi' (sushi-inspired *smørrebrød*) is a speciality.

⑦ RESTAURANT MAVEN
Nikolaj Plads 12; tel: 32 20 11 00; www.restaurantmaven.dk; Mon–Sat 11.30am–midnight, Fri–Sat until 2am; €€
This bistro opened in 2011 to instant acclaim. It serves well-presented French-Danish food in a delightfully romantic setting inside a former church.

⑧ KROGS FISKERESTAURANT
Gammel Strand 38; tel: 33 15 89 15; www.krogs.dk; Mon–Sat noon–3pm, 6–10pm; €€€€
Booking is essential if you wish to dine at Copenhagen's oldest and most expensive fish restaurant. The elegant interior dates from 1910, the six-course evening menu starts at 695dkk.

Bishop Absalon. It dates from 1901 and is the work of Danish sculptors Christian Gottlieb Vilhelm Bissen, who cast the figure, and Martin Nyrop, who was responsible for the plinth. Walk down and, to your right, you will find **Gammel Strand** (Old Beach) where, from early days, fishermen used to bring in their herring catches and their wives (the 'fishwives') sold them. **Fiskerkonen**, a statue of a sturdy fishwife by Christian Svejstrup Madsen, dates from 1940 and usually stands on the corner of the steps down to the canal that still separates the Old Town from Slotsholmen *(see p.76)*; however, she had been temporarily removed at the time of writing due to construction work on the new Metro system. In 1940 there was still a regular fish market here.

If you are hungry for a solid, proper, delicious lunch, one of the city's most renowned fish restaurants, **Krogs**, see ⑪⑧, is located on Gammel Strand. On the other side of the canal, the porticoed building is the palace church, **Christiansborg Slotskirke** *(see p.78)* and to the right of that, the ochre building is the **Thorvaldsen's Museum** *(see p.78)*. Looking ahead and to the left from the statue of Absalon, the copper roofs and twisting spire belong to the Renaissance **Børsen**, the old Stock Exchange *(see p.77)*. The spire to the left is **Holmens Kirke**, the old navy church *(see p.76)*.

Before turning back, cross to the middle of the bridge and look over the left side down to the water where you will see eight figures with their hands outstretched pleadingly beneath the surface. This little-known figure group depicts part of the legend of **Agnete and the Merman**, a story in which peasant girl Agnete marries a merman and has seven sons but then fails to return after visiting her home village. The work of Suste Bonnén, the sculpture was renovated and reinstalled here in 2007.

CHURCH OF ST NICHOLAS

Walk back up towards Strøget and take a right down Lille Kirkestræde

Royal Copenhagen

Royal Copenhagen, the Danish manufacturer of hand-made and hand-painted porcelain, was founded in 1775 by Frantz Müller, a chemist who had succeeded in mastering the difficult art of Chinese-style hard-paste porcelain. Its first designs – 'Blue Fluted', dating from 1775, based on Chinese floral motifs and 'Blue Flower', which is a little more naturalistic and dates from 1779 – were in cobalt blue, the only colour to withstand the high firing temperatures required. Its most ambitious design, 'Flora Danica', shows copies of botanical drawings and was originally commissioned by the king for Catherine the Great in 1790. The 1,802 pieces in the range took 12 years for one artist to paint. All three designs are still in production today.

Gammel Strand Antique Market

The Danes love a bargain, and Copenhagen is home to several summer flea markets. The Gammel Strand market (tel: 35 26 19 21; May–Sept: Fri–Sat 8am–5pm) is one of the most exclusive – think fine china and tasteful glassware, rather than scruffy clothes and plastic toys.

to the **Church of St Nicholas** ❿ (Sankt Nikolaj Kirke; Nikolaj Plads 10; tel: 33 18 17 80; www.kunsthallen nikolaj.dk; Tue–Sun noon–5pm; charge), named after the patron saint of sailors – an apt sponsor in a seaboard town. The mother church of the Reformation in 1536, it survived the 1728 fire, but was not so lucky in 1795 when everything but the tower was razed to the ground. Rebuilt in rather imposing red brick in the early 20th century, it is now an exhibition hall for modern art.

Food and Drink 🍴

⑨ L'ALSACE
Ny Østergade 9; tel: 33 14 57 43; www.alsace.dk; Mon–Sat 11.30am–midnight; €–€€€€
Gourmet food from Continental Europe, specialising in Alsace, in attractive surroundings. A three-course lunch menu at 320dkk is good value.

⑩ A.C. PERCH THEHANDEL
Kronprinsessgade 5; tel: 33 15 35 77; www.perchstearoom.dk; Mon–Fri 11.30am–5.30pm, Sat 11am–5pm; €€
This teashop has barely changed since 1835 and it offers an astonishing variety of teas. There's also a deliciously tea-centric café on the first floor.

⑪ CAFE HOVEDTELEGRAFEN
Købmagergade 37; tel: 33 41 09 86; www.cafehovedtelgrafen.dk; daily 10am–4pm, kitchen shuts an hour earlier; €
This rooftop café offers an airy interior and an outdoor terrace overlooking the rooftops of the old town. Snacks and main meals (mainly fish) are good.

ON TO KØBMAGERGADE

Cross over Store Kirkestraede back onto Strøget. Turn right down to Kristen Bernikows Gade and cross the road (to your right you will see the back of Magasin du Nord *(see p.43)* and a small flower market. Continue until you reach a sign-posted archway for **Pistolstræde** ⓫. Walk to the end, past various smart shops, until you reach the little courtyard with **L'Alsace**, see 🍴⑨ (which has hosted Pope John Paul II and Elton John no less), where you will see the timbered backs of 17th-century houses; unusual in an Old Town that has succumbed to two major fires.

Walk through to Grønnegade, a pretty street (look at the houses to your right) and turn left, then right back on to Kristen Bernikows Gade. Take the first left on to Sværtergade: the little yellow building on the right, con-

Right: exhibit at the Post & Tele Museum.

structed immediately after the first fire, is the smallest house in the old town. One block further, Sværtergade turns into Kronprinsensgade, one of Copenhagen's poshest shopping streets (even if it does have a 7/11 on the corner). **Summerbird Chocolaterie** (Kronprinsensgade 11; tel: 33 93 80 40), another well-known chocolate maker, can be found along here, as can Copenhagen's oldest teashop, **A.C. Perch Thehandel**, see ⑪⑩, at No. 5.

At the end, turn right onto Købmagergade. Opposite you is the **Post & Tele Museum** and further down on your right, the **Round Tower**; **Trinity Church** next to it; and, opposite, **Regensen** ⑫, a 17th-century student hall of residence, which is still in use.

Post & Tele Museum

Copenhagen's main post office is home to the **Post & Tele Museum** ⑬ (Købmagergade 37; tel: 33 41 09 00; www.ptt-museum.dk; daily 10am– 4pm; free), which charts the history of communication from the 17th century. Even though labelling is mostly in Danish, it makes for an interesting browse. Ignore the stamp collection and head up to **Café Hovedtelegrafen** for excellent views, see ⑪⑪.

Round Tower

Continue down Købmagergade until you see the **Round Tower** (Rundetårn) ⑭ (Kobmagergade 52a; tel: 33 73 03 73; www.rundetaarn.dk; Oct–May: daily 10am–5pm; June–Sept: daily 10am–8pm; also mid-Oct–mid-Mar Tue & Wed 7–10pm; charge), the

round red-brick tower on your right. This unusual building is a 17th-century observatory, the oldest in Europe, built by Christian IV and thought to be mentioned in H.C. Andersen's fairytale of the *Soldier and the Tinder Box* where a dog is described as having 'eyes as big as a tower'.

Andersen knew this tower well and, as an observatory, it was literally an 'eye' on the heavens. Inside, a wide cobbled ramp spirals up through the tower, designed for a horse and cart to use (the only practical way of taking heavy equipment all the way to the top). In 1716, Tsar Peter of Russia

Streets off Strøget

Although this walk takes in the major sights, don't be afraid to wander down streets that take your fancy; there are many treasures (historical and retail) around almost every corner. Unexpected finds are part of the pleasure of ambling around this area. North and south of Strøget, the streets offer more individual shopping in little one-off boutiques, record and second-hand shops. Streets to head for include Skindergade, Larsbjørnstræde and the three parrallel streets: Vestergade, Studiestræde, Sankt Peders Stræde; and Læderstræde and Kompagnistræde, which run into each other; the latter is especially good for antiques shops.

Stargazing
The Round Tower was once the tallest building in Copenhagen and houses Europe's oldest observatory. It was used by astronomers at the University of Copenhagen until 1861.

Below: spa at First Hotel Sankt Petri.

himself galloped his horse to the top of the 209m (686ft) ramp inside the Round Tower, followed more sedately by his wife in a carriage. Now there is a yearly unicycle race to the top and back, usually held in May. There is also an art gallery, formerly the university library, about half way up.

Trinity Church
Next door is **Trinity Church** ⓯ (Trinitatis Kirke; Købmagergade 52a/Landemærket 12; tel: 33 37 65 40; www.trinitatiskirke.dk; Mon–Sat 9.30am–4.30pm), commissioned as the university church by Christian IV, and finished in 1657 under Frederik III.

Although the Round Tower survived the blaze of 1728, the church suffered. Its roof and the university library that lay beneath it were charred to a crisp and its interior damaged. But it was quickly restored by 1731 and is now a lovely white-and-gold Rococo affair with a splendid Baroque altar-piece, a three-faced Rococo clock, a vaulted roof picked out in gold, galleries running down both side walls and a fabulous gold- and silver-coloured organ. If it is open, it is worth a visit; otherwise, look down the nave through a glass panel as you start up the Round Tower.

KRYSTALGADE

Continue and turn left up Krystalgade, the spire of the Church of Our Lady (Vor Frue Kirke) in view. The large red-brick building set behind grey railings a little way up on your right is Copenhagen's **Grand Synagogue** ⓰ (Synagogen; usually closed to the public). The centre for Judaism in Denmark, it dates from 1883 and, amazingly, survived the Nazi occupation. Its interior is notable for Egyptian-influenced elements. Its sacred Torah scrolls were hidden in Trinity Church during World War II.

Cross over Filostræde. The back of the university building is on your left (you can see the book stacks through the windows) and the **First Hotel Sankt Petri**, see ⑪⑫, where you can settle down for an early evening cocktail, is a little further up, also on your right.

NØRREGADE

At the end of the street, take a left onto Nørregade. On your right is the **Church of St Peter ⑰**.

Church of St Peter

The first Church of St Peter (Sankt Petri Kirke; Larslejsstæde 11; tel: 33 13 38 33; Mar–mid-Oct: Tue–Sat 11am–3pm) was built here in around 1200 in the Romanesque style. It burnt down and was replaced, *c*.1450, with a Gothic structure, minus the transepts, which were added in the 17th century.

During the Reformation, the church was deconsecrated and turned into a canon foundry, but in 1585 it was reinstated and given to the German-speaking population by Frederik II. German was the main language spoken by the court and, as a result, Sankt Petri became an important intellectual, economic and political meeting place.

The fire of 1728 destroyed its interior, and new decoration, including the Baroque main entrance (1730s) and the copper-clad spire (1757), were introduced. Its vaulted sepulchral chapel (1681–83), which has some impressive statuary, is the resting place of the royal architect Nicolai Eigtved (1701–54), who designed the church spire; and possibly of the German doctor Johann Struensee (1737–72), who stepped into the king's shoes and ruled Denmark for over a year *(see p.79)*.

The University

On your left, as you walk towards the Church of Our Lady, there is a square. The building facing the side of the

Above from far left: the café at the First Hotel Sankt Petri; the Absolut Icebar draws crowds to Hotel 27 on Løngangstræde; the unique ramp inside the Round Tower.

Food and Drink

⑫ BAR ROUGE: FIRST HOTEL SANKT PETRI
Krystalgade 22; tel: 33 45 91 00; www.hotelsktpetri.com; open from 5pm; €€€
As evening draws in, head for Bar Rouge (located at the top of the escalators inside Hotel Sankt Petri). It's famous for its cocktails, from classics to their own creations such as the champagne-based Strawberry Summer, which is guaranteed to induce a holiday mood.

Royal Weddings

When Crown Prince Frederik married Australian commoner Mary Donaldson in May 2004, walking her down the aisle of the Church of Our Lady (Vor Frue Kirke), he was following in the footsteps of some of his forebears: Queen Margrethe I who, at the age of nine, married the Norwegian king Haakan in 1363; and Christian I who married his queen, Dorothea, here in 1449. The Danish monarchy holds the record for unbroken succession from the Viking chief Gorm the Old, father of Harald Bluetooth, who died in *c*.958, of fifty kings (predominantly named Frederik or Christian) and two queens, both Margrethe – the second celebrates her 40th Jubilee in 2012.

The Bells of St Mary's

The 60m-high tower of the Church of Our Lady contains four bells. One, dating to 1490, is the oldest in the country. Another, named 'Stormk-lokken', is the heaviest bell in Denmark, weighing a hefty 4 tons.

Below: the light and bright interior of the Church of Our Lady.

church is the **University ⑱** (Universitet). There has been a university in Copenhagen since 1479 and it currently educates around 37,000 students. It was located on the corner of Nørregade and Studiestræde until just after the Reformation in 1536, when it was moved across the street to the vacated Bishops Palace.

The fires of 1728 and 1795 and the British Navy bombardment in 1807 made short work of any ancient buildings and the current one dates from the 19th century. The portrait busts are of illustrious professors.

Church of Our Lady

There has been a church on the site of the cathedral, the **Church of Our Lady ⑲** (Vor Frue Kirke; Nørregade, Vor Frue Plads, tel: 33 37 65 40; daily 8am–5pm), is the latest in a line of church buildings dating back to 1209. Fires destroyed two of the earlier churches, the British bombardment of 1807 destroyed when the navy used the church spire as a target. The current building, designed by C.F. Hansen, dates from 1829 and only the tower and the walls of the side aisles remain of the medieval building. The front door is guarded by towering statues of **King David** and **Moses**, while the interior is noteworthy for its reliefs and imposing marble statues by Bertel Thorvaldsen *(see p.78)*, dating from 1839. These include **Christ and the 12 Apostles** (with Judas replaced by St Paul) on the altar and along the side walls; and the beautiful angel holding a shell, which serves as the cathedral's font.

Outside the cathedral, the **monument** on Bispetorvet commemorates the 400th anniversary of the Reformation. Cross the square and head down Studiestræde opposite the Church of Our Lady, past **The Living Room**, see ⑪⑬. Take a left at the next junction and a short walk will bring you back to Rådhuspladsen.

THE HARBOUR AREA

This walk is a short but colourful one, starting in Kongens Nytorv (King's New Square), the height of 17th-century aristocratic elegance, and leading down to Nyhavn. Once known for its brothels and seedy taverns, today the harbour is a popular outdoor area with lots of attractive restaurants and bars.

In the Middle Ages, Kongens Nytorv, an elegant square that now seems integral to Copenhagen, was outside the city walls and quite a way from the banks of the Sound. It began to develop under Frederik III (1648–70). In 1671–73, his son Christian V (1670–99) commissioned a canal (now called Nyhavn, or 'New Harbour') to be dug from the Sound to the square so that merchant ships could sail inland and unload their cargo more easily. He also ordered landowners with property bordering on the square to build grand mansions or to sell their land to someone who would.

DISTANCE 1km (½ mile)
TIME 1hr (plus boat trip 1hr)
START Hôtel d'Angleterre
END Nyhavn
POINTS TO NOTE
If you don't take a harbour cruise, this is a nice walk to do at the end of the day, ending on Nyhavn for a drink or dinner. If you walk up one of the side streets onto Sankt Annae Plads, it connects easily with the walk of the Royal District *(see p.47).*

KONGENS NYTORV

Standing at the bottom of **Strøget** *(see p.32)* you face Kongens Nytorv with Nyhavn (out of sight) lying on the far side of the square. To your left, at the corner of the square is Copenhagen's swankiest hotel, the **Hôtel d'Angleterre**; to your right the building with the fancy cupola is **Magasin du Nord**, the city's oldest department store.

Hôtel d'Angleterre

The **Hôtel d'Angleterre ❶** reopened its doors in 2012 after extensive refurbishment. It has seen its fair share of wealthy visitors since opening its doors in 1755. Guests have included H.C. Andersen, Grace Kelly, Winston Churchill, Margaret Thatcher, Bill Clinton, Woody Allen, Pierce Brosnan and Madonna. When Michael Jackson stayed in the 1980s, he was so enthralled by some of its furnishings that he wanted to buy them; when politely told they were not for sale, he offered to buy the entire hotel instead. Oddly enough, they declined.

Magasin du Nord

Originally a hotel, the **Magasin du Nord ❷**, dates from the 19th century. At Vingårdstræde 6 is an attic room where H.C. Anderson lived while he was studying for his exams in 1827. The

Above: the front door of the Hôtel d'Angleterre; Magasin du Nord is the city's biggest department store.

Above from left: Kunsthal Charlottenborg is the venue for changing exhibitions of contemporary Danish and international art; picturesque Nyhavn; the crimson-and-gold Royal Theatre.

department store is also a good stop for a coffee or bite to eat in an area where you pay for the location.

The Royal Theatre and Kunsthal Charlottenborg

The **Royal Theatre** ❸ (Det Kongelige Teater; *see p.20*) stands opposite the Magasin du Nord on the south side of the square. There has been a theatre here since 1748; the present theatre was built in the 1870s, taking the classically inspired Parisian Opera as its model. It has been somewhat eclipsed by the new Royal Danish Playhouse *(see p.20)*. Pop down August Bournonvilles Passage, to the side of the theatre, to see the 1930s mosaic ceiling in the archway.

East of the theatre is **Kunsthal Charlottenborg** ❹ (tel: 33 36 90 50; www.kunsthalcharlottenborg.dk; Tue–Sun 11am–5pm, Wed until 8pm; charge), built in the 17th century as a palatial residence for Frederik III's illegitimate son Ulrik. Less than a century later, it became the Royal Danish Academy of Fine Arts, where painters, sculptors and architects learned their trade. It is now used for contemporary art exhibitions.

Hans Christian Andersen Andersen always loved the Royal Theatre and liked to live close by. He wrote his first fairytales, including *The Tinder Box* and *The Princess and the Pea*, in 1835 when he lived at no. 20 (then 289) Nyhavn. In winter, the house was so cold that his landlady's children poured water on the floor to make ice slides.

Equestrian Statue of Christian V

Look to the centre of the square where you will see a large **equestrian statue of Christian V** ❺ dressed as a Roman emperor, riding over the fallen figure of Envy. The king is surrounded by Queen Artemisia, Alexander the Great, the goddess Pallas Athene and Hercules. Sculpted by the Frenchman Abraham César Lamoureux, it was the first equestrian statue in Scandinavia and was originally made of gilded lead because bronze castings of this size were not possible at the time. It has been repaired many times and in 1946 was recast in bronze. The original can now be found in Christian IV's Brewery (Bryghus; *see p.80*).

NYHAVN

At the bottom of Kongens Nytorv lies the 'New Harbour' or **Nyhavn** ❻, lined with pastel-coloured, merchants' houses that date from when the canal was constructed. Their warehouses stood at the end; a couple still survive and are now smart, boutique hotels, The Admiral and 71 Nyhavn *(see p.114)*.

With its attractive historical ships

Food and Drink 🍴

① **CAP HORN**

Nyhavn 21; tel: 33 12 85 04; www.caphorn.dk; daily 9am–1am (lunch 11.30am–5pm; kitchen open until 11pm); €€

Nyhavn eateries are more about people-watching than food, but this appealing place serves good grub too, including lamb, deer and duck dishes, and some lighter fish mains.

at anchor, Nyhavn is not just of interest for its 17th- and 18th-century mariners' past. From the 1880s, it was also the gateway to a new life in the US, since it was here that you bought your ticket from one of the many shipping offices that sprang up. A new start for many, although not for the 14 unfortunates who set sail to join the Titanic's maiden voyage in 1912 of whom only two survived.

The entrance to Nyhavn is heralded by a large **anchor**, honouring 1,600 Danish sailors who lost their lives in World War II. To the left as you face the Sound is the **Amber Museum** ❼ (Kongens Nytorv 2; tel: 33 11 67 00; www.houseofamber.com; Oct–Apr: daily 10am–6pm, May–Sept: daily 10am–7pm; charge) showcasing Denmark's national gemstone. When you learn that most amber deposits weigh 10g (½oz) or less each, you will understand the wonder of the chunk weighing a record-breaking 8.8kg (19lbs 6oz) that they have on display.

Nyhavn's North Side

This 'sunny side' of the canal is a popular restaurant area; sit inside or out (blankets and heaters are provided in winter), but grab a seat while you can, as it is almost always busy. The restaurants are all in old buildings and have names such as Skipperkroen (the Skipper's Inn), **Cap Horn**, see ⑪①, or La Sirène (the Siren); they are linked to the lives and travels of the sailors who used to saunter along here looking for women, drink, a bed and possibly a fight.

Hans Christian Andersen spent around 22 years lodging at various addresses in Nyhavn, including **Nos 18**, **20** and **67**.

Above: the equestrian statue of Christian V; artwork in front of the Kunsthal Charlottenborg.

Ahoy Sailor!
Sailors have all but disappeared from Nyhavn. In the past, there was an average of 22,000 sailors from all over the world in the city at any one time, and it was not uncommon for ships to dock for two weeks. Nowadays ships often put in for less than a day.

Left: capturing the beauty of Nyhavn.

Side Streets

The side streets off Nyhavn are well worth a look and, like the harbour itself, have come up in the world. The first turning on your left takes you up **Store Strandstræde** (Big Beach Street), the only remnant of its seafaring past is a tatoo parlour that claims to have been on the site since the 16th century.

There's a nice little restaurant called **Zeleste**, see ⑪②, along here – you'll recognise it by the kitsch, plastic crayfish hanging outside.

Continue along and at the end turn right, back on yourself, down **Lille Strandstræde** (Little Beach Street), also home to small galleries and designer clothes shops. If you are looking for a cheap sandwich, pop into **Thomas Sandwich Bar**, see ③. Carry on to the end and you will find yourself back on Nyhavn.

Boat Trips Round the Harbour

If you want to take a boat trip through the harbour area, which is highly recommended, you will find the **DFDS** tour boats ❽ at the top of Nyhavn near the anchor, and the **Netto Bådene** boats ❾ further along the south side of the canal. The blue-and-yellow local transport boats also stop at the jetty at the end of Nyhavn. Seeing the city from the water is a great way to understand the layout of this waterside city, which began on the island of Slotsholmen.

On such a trip, you would expect to go up the harbour, passing by the Royal Danish Playhouse (*see p.20*); the new **Opera House** (*see p.86*); and **Langelinie**, **Kastellet** and *The Little Mermaid* (*see p.51*). Some tours head further out to **Trekroner**, an 18th-century fort used once in 1801 against the British, before turning back to sail past **Christianshavn** (*see p.82*), down the **Frederiksberg Kanal**, then past **Slotsholmen** (*see p.76*) and the royal palace, the **Bryghus**, the **Black Diamond** and **Holmens Kirke** and back to Nyhavn.

Food and Drink 🍴

② ZELESTE

Store Strandstraede 6; tel: 33 16 06 06; open daily 10.30am–11pm; kitchen open 11am–9pm; www.zeleste.dk; €–€€

Pretty whitewashed restaurant with cobbled courtyard. Hearty menu changes regularly. Great brunches. Book to avoid disappointment.

③ THOMAS SANDWICH BAR

Lille Strandstraede 17; tel: 33 13 13 31; €

Tiny basement eatery with room for a handful of people. Makes excellent fresh savoury sandwiches.

THE ROYAL DISTRICT

*This walk takes you through Copenhagen's grandest quarter, Frederiksstaden,
and then along the banks of the Sound. Once a heaving commercial and
naval area, its quiet streets are now frequented by tourists and locals,
including the royal family, who live at Amalienborg palace at its heart.*

In 1749, Frederik V laid the foundation stone for his building project, the Frederiksstad, a grand court district adorned with a large and beautiful church rivalling almost anything else in Europe. He was an absolute monarch, belonging to the 300-year-old Oldenburg dynasty and wanted to create something startling; and he did. He even got his wealthy subjects to pay for it.

The rococo palaces of the Amalienborg were designed for four aristocratic families in the 1750s by royal architect Nicolai Eigtved. Several decades later, the royal family moved in, and Amalienborg is still their winter home.

Start at Sankt Annæ Plads **❶**, a tree-lined boulevard created during the building of Frederiksstaden, when a former canal was filled in. A large **equestrian statue of Christian X** (1912–47) presides over the top end of the 'square', while the harbour end is dominated by the Royal Danish Playhouse *(see p.20)*. Close to the statue is the **Garrison's Church ❷** (Garnisons Kirke; Tue–Fri 9am–1pm; free) and its graveyard, built to replace the castle chapel that burned down in 1689 *(see p.48)*. Copenhagen's garrison attended church here from 1706. The plain

> **DISTANCE** 4km (2½ miles)
> **TIME** A half day
> **START** Sankt Annæ Plads
> **END** Kongens Nytorv
> **POINTS TO NOTE**
> Most of the food options are towards
> the end of the walk near Bredgade,
> which makes this a good choice for
> a morning walk. Alternatively, have a
> picnic by the Sound or in Kastellet.

white interior is composed of unusual two-storey galleries, with a dramatic black altarpiece (1724) providing the main focus of attention.

AMALIENBORG

From here, cross the square and turn left up **Amaliegade**. There are several embassies along here and the buildings are some of the most elegant and

> # Food and Drink
> **① RESTAURANT AMALIE**
> Amaliegade 11; tel: 33 12
> 88 10; Mon–Sat 11.30am–4pm; €€
> This excellent wood-panelled, can-
> dlelit lunch restaurant serves up
> delicious Danish *smørrebrød*. Good
> value for the quality.

Above: Sankt Annæ Plads; one of the 14 Danish 'Fathers of the Church' outside the Marble Church.

Amaliegade Residents
Before he became a 'Prince of Denmark' in 1852, at the age of 34, Christian IX *(see p.49)* lived with his family in a yellow town house at Amaliegade 18. Four of his children were born there between 1843 and 1847.

Changing the Guard
The Amalienborg is guarded by the Royal Life Guards who do two-hour shifts. When the queen is in residence, they are replaced at noon by the guards from the Rosenborg Palace.

expensive in the city. If you need a bite to eat check out **Restaurant Amalie**, see ⑪①, or the equally popular **Café Toldboden**, see ⑪② *(see p.49)*. Go through the arch that leads into the grandest part of the Frederiksstad, the square around which the four palaces of the **Amalienborg ❸** stand.

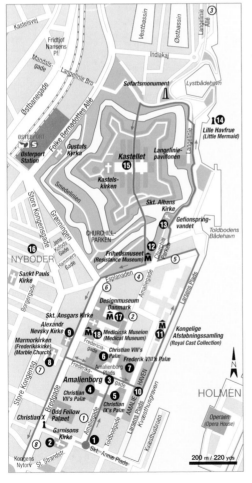

The Palaces

The palace complex Amalienborg was built on the site of a previous palace which burned down in a horrific fire: during a theatrical performance on 19 April 1689 for Christian V's birthday, part of the stage set caught alight and 180 people died in the blaze.

In 1794, the royal family moved in after a fire at Slotsholmen *(see p.76)*, and liked their new home so much that the king purchased all four buildings. They have lived here ever since, members often occupying each palace at different times.

As you stand in the centre of the octagonal 'square' looking back at the colonnade, the palace to your right is **Christian VII's palace ❹** (Christian VII's Palæ; entrance by guided tour, in English July–Sept Sat–Sun 1pm & 2.30pm; charge), one of the first to be finished before Eigtved died in 1754. This was originally the sumptuous home of Lord High Steward Adam Gottlob Moltke and the most expensive of the four; it is widely considered to be Denmark's best rococo interior. Christian VII, who was schizophrenic, lived here from December 1794 until his death in 1808. The queen now uses it to welcome foreign dignitaries.

On the left of the colonnade, which connects the two palaces, you'll find **Christian IX's Palace ❺** (Christian IX's Palæ), which is home to Queen Margrethe and Prince Henrik, and was originally known as Schack's Palace. Crown Prince Frederik VI and his wife Marie were the first Royals

to move in and lived here for over 40 years. Frederik was Regent and ruled for his father from 1784–1808. Even so, he often needed his father's signature for affairs of state, so he had the colonnade built between the two palaces, with a corridor running through it for easy access.

Turn your back on these palaces and the palace on your left is **Christian VIII's Palace** (Christian VIII's Palæ), originally called the Levetzau Palace. Part of the palace is open all year as a **museum** to the Glücksberg dynasty (tel: 33 12 08 08; www.amalienborgmuseet.dk; Nov–21 Dec and Jan–Apr: Tue–Sun 11am–4pm; May–Oct: daily 10am–4pm; guided tours in English, French, German and Danish; separate tours of the Bel-étage: every second week, Wed and Sun 11.30am, 1pm, 2.30pm; charge). Here, you can see the chintzy drawing room of Queen Louise and the studies of Frederik VIII, Frederik IX, Christian IX, and Christian X, which have all been moved from other parts of the Amalienborg.

On your right is **Frederik VIII's Palace** ❼ (Frederik VIII's Palæ), with a clock on its facade, which is the home of Crown Prince Frederik and his Australian wife, the Crown Princess Mary Donaldson.

In the centre of the square is an equestrian statue of **Frederik V**, dressed as a Roman emperor. Sculptor Jacques Saly took over 20 years to complete the statue owing, it is said, to his commitment to having fun, hence the delay. It was unveiled in 1771 with a 21-gun salute.

The Marble Church

You will see the spectacular **Marble Church** ❽ (Marmorkirken; Frederiksgade 4; tel: 33 15 01 44; www.marmorkirken.dk; Mon, Tue, Thur, Sat 10am–5pm; Wed 10am–6.30pm; Fri–Sun noon–5pm; free, but charge to climb dome) or, more properly,

---

Food and Drink

② CAFE TOLDBODEN
Amaliegade 41; tel: 33 12 94 67; Mon–Fri 11am–3pm; €€€
Join the local suits who stop for their lunchtime *smørrebrød* in this 18th-century town house. Book to be sure of a seat.

Father-in-Law of Europe

Christian IX (1863–1906), for whom one of the Amalienborg palaces is named, came to be known as the 'father-in-law of Europe' because his six children married into the royal families of Sweden, Britain, Russia, Germany and France. A nephew of the childless Frederik VII (1848–63), he was the first king since Christian I (1448–81) not to succeed his father or grandfather, and, although a choice favoured by the Danes, he was not the nearest legal heir. Christian improved his claim by marrying Louise of Hesse, who was more closely related on the female side. His daughter Alexandra married King Edward VII of Britain (who reigned 1901–10), son of Queen Victoria.

'Frederikskirke' (after the monarch), if you stand with your back to the statue. It was designed as a very important part of the Frederiksstad by Nicolai Eigtved in 1740; yet, 30 years on, it remained unfinished and funds had run out. It languished in ruins for over a century when help came in the guise of an industrialist, Carl Frederik Tietgen, and it was inaugurated in August 1894. A massive dome stands on 12 pillars and is covered in paintings of the 12 apostles, light flooding in from 12 skylights. At 31m (101ft) in diameter, the dome is second only in size to that of St Peter's in Rome, which measures 42m (137ft). You can go up at 1pm and 3pm (daily mid-June–Aug, Sat–Sun rest of year) for some wonderful views.

Outside, at ground level, there are 14 Danish 'Fathers of the Church' and higher up, 18 figures of prophets, apostles and figures from Church history, finishing with Martin Luther.

Alexander Nevsky Church

Coming out of the church, look to your left up Bredgade (an exclusive street full of antique shops and auction houses): you will see the golden onion domes of **Alexander Nevsky Church** ❾ (Alexandr Nevsky Kirke; Bredgade 53; tel: 20 76 16 47 for group visits; Wed 11.30am–1.30pm), a Russian orthodox church, built in 1883 as a gift from Tsar Alexander III to mark his marriage to Princess Marie Dagmar.

Walk back to the Amalienborg and through the square to the waterside, where you will find **Amalie Haven** ❿, a pretty park directly across from the **Opera House** *(see p.86)*.

Marie Dagmar

Marie Dagmar, the second daughter of Christian IX, married the future Tsar Alexander III in St Petersburg in 1866. She had, in fact, been betrothed to Alexander's brother Nicholas in 1864 but he had died suddenly of tuberculous meningitis a few months after their engagement. She became known as Maria Feodorovna and had four sons and two daughters including Tsar Nicholas II and the Grand Duke Michael who were both murdered during the Russian Revolution in 1918. She escaped to London in 1919 and

eventually returned to Denmark where she died in 1928. Her funeral was held at Alexander Nevsky Church and she was buried in Roskilde Cathedral where she remained until 2005, when her remains were returned to St Petersburg, as she had wished, to be buried next to her husband.

ALONG THE HARBOUR

Walk along the harbourside, chimneys and windmills visible in the distance, until you reach a copy of Michelangelo's statue of *David*. This heralds the **Royal Cast Collection** ⓫ (Den Kongelige Afstøbningssamling; Vestindisk Pakhus, Toldbodgade 40; tel: 33 74 84 84 (10am–2pm); www.smk.dk; Tue 10am–4pm, Sun 2pm–5pm; free). Set in an 18th-century warehouse, there are copies of over 2,000 famous statues charting the history of sculpture from Ancient Egypt and antiquity onwards.

Walk for another 250m (270 yards) along the harbourside until you see the green-topped pavilions on the quayside. It is from here that the royal family take a tender when boarding their yacht *Dannebrøg*. Turn left onto **Esplanaden**, which used to be a busy thoroughfare between the docks and **Nyboder**, Christian IV's naval housing estate built in 1631 *(see p.52)*. Turning right along Churchillparken, you will find the **Frihedsmuseet** (Resistance Museum); the 19th-century mockgothic English **Church of St Albans**; and the fountain *Gefionspringvandet*.

The Resistance Museum

The **Resistance Museum** 🔟 (Frihedsmuseet; Churchillparken 7; tel: 33 47 39 21; www.natmus.dk; May–Sept: Tue–Sun 10am–5pm; Oct–Apr: Tue–Sun 10am–3pm; free) charts the activities of the Resistance during the German Occupation in 1940–45, including sabotage, underground press and the rescue of most of Denmark's Jewish population. Film and recorded interviews and personal memorabilia, including letters and toys, make the period come alive. An execution post is a horrible reminder of the dangers that these people ran.

Gefionspringvandet Statue

Commissioned by Carl Jacobsen, the **statue** 🔟 on top of this dramatic fountain (inaugurated in 1909) shows the goddess Gefion driving a plough and four oxen at great speed. She had tricked the Swedish king, who did not know her identity, into letting her have

as much land as she could plough in one night, so she transformed her four giant sons and ploughed enough land to create the island of Sjælland (Zealand).

TOWARDS THE LITTLE MERMAID

Now cross over the bridge behind the *Gefion* fountain back to the waterside. To your left you will see the grassy ramparts of **Kastellet**, which you can visit later.

Along the quayside are various statues. The first on your left is of Frederik IX (1947–72), Queen Margrethe's father; a little further on is a bronze bust of one Princess Marie, who died young, hence the mourning mother and child at the base of the statue. Just before you reach *The Little Mermaid*, you will see a tall pillar, topped by a winged Victory, with cannons and canonballs at its base. This is *Huitfeldt Søjlen* (The Huitfeldt Column), which commemorates Ivar Huitfeldt, a naval captain who died saving many ships in the battle of Køge Bay against the Swedes in 1710.

Continue on and you will most likely come to a group of tourists; behind them you will find *The Little Mermaid* 🔟 (Lille Havfrue), commissioned by the Carlsberg Foundation in 1909. Edvard Eriksen's small, gentle figure staring out to sea was modelled on his wife Eline. It dates from 1913. Just beyond is another Carlsberg commission, *Efter Badet* (After the Bath). Another winged woman (based on an ancient statue of Nike from Samothrace) looks out over the marina from the *Søfartsmonumentet*,

Above from far left: the dome of the Marble Church was inspired by St Peter's in Rome; statues of prophets and apostles surround the dome; the powerful oxen of *Gefionspringvandet*; the unmistakable domes of Alexandr Nevsky Church.

Below: battered armoured car at the Resistance Museum; the Marble Church dome and statue.

Above from left: the church in Kastellet; the Designmuseum Danmark explores different themes in both Danish and international design; typical ochre-coloured house in Nyboder.

created in 1928 in memory of Danish merchant ships and sailors who perished at sea. This walk now turns back towards the city centre; but if you are peckish, walk around the marina to **Café Langelinie**, see ⑪③; and if you're feeling flush, the Langelinie Outlet Stores are just beyond the café on the quay.

Kastellet

Follow Langelinie round, cross the bridge, with the marina on your right, and go down the steps to **Kastellet ⑮**, Copenhagen's star-shaped fort, dating from 1662. Over 350 years later, it is still being used by the military. Nonetheless, it is a delightfully peaceful enclave, with 17th- and 18th-century buildings including a church, prison, the commander's house and a gatehouse. There's a charming **windmill** and the grassy ramparts (open 6am–10pm) are pleasant to walk around, even if the building interiors are off limits to civilians.

Towards Nyboder

Walk through Kastellet and you will come back on to Esplanaden near the Resistance Museum. Just opposite stop for a well-earned coffee at **Kafferiet**, see ⑪④, a small coffee shop in a pale-blue, 18th-century town house. If you are looking for something a bit more substantial, turn left up Esplanaden towards the harbour until you reach **Lumskebugten**, see ⑪⑤.

If you want to have a look at **Nyboder ⑯**, carry on down Esplanaden, away from the harbour, until you reach the grid of ochre-coloured houses. The area's distinctive homes were built by Christian IV in response to a desperate housing shortage for navy personnel. The single-storeyed houses date back to 1631; the two-storeyed date from the 18th century and the grey-brick buildings are from the 19th century.

Otherwise turn left down Bredgade, where you will find **Café Petersborg**,

The Little Mermaid
The Little Mermaid has suffered many indignities in her time, including having her head chopped off – twice. Now, controversial artist Bjørn Norgaard has produced *The Genetically Modified Little Mermaid* (2008), a grotesque sculpture that poses on a similar rock 400m (1312ft) from the long-suffering original.

see ⑪⑥, on your left or take the next left onto Store Kongensgade for a Copenhagen institution, **Restaurant Ida Davidsen**, see ⑪⑦. Just down on your left you'll find two fascinating museums, the **Designmuseum Danmark** and the **Medical Museum**.

Designmuseum Danmark

Set in Frederiksstad's former hospital (1754–1910), the **Designmuseum Danmark** ⑰ (Bredgade 68; tel: 33 18 56 56; www.designmuseum.dk; Tue–Sun 11am–5pm; charge, under-18s free, Wed free) is an interesting journey through the history of household design. From Harley Davidsons to cardboard chairs, oriental medieval handicrafts to rococo furniture, you will be hard pushed not to find something appealing. Most of the information is in Danish but you can appreciate what you see without too much information. It also has a pretty garden and an indoor café with good cakes.

The Medical Museum

The **Medical Museum** ⑱ (Medicinsk Museion; Bredgade 62; tel: 35 32 38 00; www.museion.ku.dk; Wed–Fri & Sun 1–5pm; guided tours July–Aug: 2.30pm; charge) is next door. Not for the squeamish, but a fascinating collection for anyone interested in the peculiarities and horrors of medicine in a bygone age.

Now walk back down to Kongens Nytorv past all the art galleries and auction houses. To end on an indulgent note, pop into **Alida Marstrand**, see ⑪⑧, one of Copenhagen's superior purveyors of hand-made Easter eggs.

Food and Drink 🍴

③ CAFÉ LANGELINIE
Langeliniekaj 5; tel: 98 63 44 43; daily 11.30am–9pm; €
Stop on the pier for cake and coffee, or a light lunch of soup, smørrebrød or fishcakes.

④ KAFFERIET
Esplanaden 44; tel:33 93 93 04; Mon–Fri 7.30am–6pm, Sat–Sun 10am–6pm; €
A cute café in a perfect duck-egg-blue townhouse. Enjoy excellent double-roast coffee in the quirky interior, illuminated by homemade lamps.

⑤ LUMSKEBUGTEN
Esplanaden 21; tel: 33 15 60 29; Mon–Sat lunch, Wed–Sat dinner; €€–€€€
Charming, airy restaurant in a former sailors' tavern given to leisurely meals. You may bump into royalty.

⑥ CAFE PETERSBORG
Bredgade 76; tel: 33 12 50 16; Mon–Fri 11.45am–4pm, 5–9pm; Sat–Sun 11.45am–4pm; €–€€
Excellent Danish café-restaurant in the beamed basement of a house dating from 1746, part of which used to house the Russian embassy. Go for a smørrebrød or a full meal.

⑦ RESTAURANT IDA DAVIDSEN
Store Kongensgade 70; tel: 33 91 36 55; Mon–Fri 10.30am–4pm; €
This pricey smørrebrød restaurant is a Copenhagen institution dating from 1888, with a choice of 250 sandwiches (although some say it has been surpassed by Aamanns, see p.59).

⑧ ALIDA MARSTRAND
Bredgade 14; tel: 33 15 13 63; Tue–Fri 11am–5pm, Sat 10am–1pm
This small chocolatier opened in 1930, with confectionery recipes gleaned from the Tzar's court.

Above: the charming windmill in Kastellet (1847); Designmuseum Danmark exhibit.

Nyboder
The inhabitants of Nyboder received free housing and education but in return all boys went to sea for 16–20 years of compulsory service. Naval law applied to the women and children as well as the men.

5 AROUND ROSENBORG

Rosenborgslot Slot seems remarkable not just for its beauty but also its position bang in the middle of Copenhagen, surrounded by elegant town houses, the botanical gardens and a couple of lovely art galleries.

DISTANCE 2km (1½ miles)

TIME A half/full day

START David Collection

END Hirschsprung Collection

POINTS TO NOTE

If you find yourself short on time, visit Rosenborg Palace and the National Gallery of Art *(see p.60)* and just walk through the King's Gardens and the botanical gardens. The latter make for a welcoming break if you have had your dose of historical artefacts and paintings.

Below: taking a stroll in the King's Gardens.

The Dutch Renaissance-style castle Rosenborg is a real highlight of the city. However, when the architect-king Christian IV built it in 1606, it actually stood outside Copenhagen, in the countryside beyond the north-eastern ramparts. Christiansborg was a crumbling mess at the time, and the royal residence of Frederiksborg lay an inconvenient 35km (22 miles) away, so it made sense to have a palace closer to the city.

Rosenborg was built in several stages *(see p.57)*; by 1624, it was much as it is today. It is still surrounded by the pretty **King's Gardens** (Kongens Have), a welcome green area, and extremely popular with Copenhageners. Around three million people come to stroll, sunbathe and picnic here each year.

The most impressive way to approach the castle is through the gardens from the Kronprinsessegade gate. However, before you go in, take half an hour or so in the **David Collection ❶** (Davids Samling; Kronprinsessegade 30–32; tel: 33 73 49 49; www.david mus.dk; Tue & Fri 1–5pm, Wed 10am–9pm, Thur 10am–5pm, Sat–Sun 11am–5pm), a lovely collection of European fine arts and Islamic and far-eastern art from the 7th to the 19th centuries, recently reopened after an extensive renovation.

The collection is housed in an old town house – worth a visit in itself – on a street that, until the fire of 1795, was part of the King's Gardens. After the fire, King Frederik VI donated a strip of land to the city and a long line of neoclassical houses was built. The sale of these financed rebuilding in the Old Town. At the same time, 12 dinky little shop-pavilions were built along the park's edge. The buildings, with a floor space of 16 sq m (53 sq ft), are still in use today.

KING'S GARDENS

From the entrance to the **King's Garden ❷** (Kongens Have; open from 7am daily, closing times vary from Jan 5pm to July 11pm; free; *see map on p.56*), you will see the best view of the turreted romantic castle, straight down the crocus lawn (finest in spring), lined with marble spheres dating from 1674. The entrance at the end, dating from 1611, is guarded by stone lions and accessed by the 'green bridge' over the moat.

Wander at will in the gardens or to see it all before visiting the castle, turn left at the entrance and walk around the edge of the park until you come to the second path on your right.

Krumspringet

Turn right and right again to visit the **Krumspringet ❹**, a maze of narrow paths arranged in a symmetrical pattern. This one is modern, but old garden plans show that there was a maze in the gardens back in the 17th century. The name comes from the Danish for 'dodge' because people could avoid unwanted meetings by nipping out of the way down one of its many paths. Walk to the centre and then out again, by the next path on the right, which will bring you to the **crocus lawn ❺**, which is truly spectacular in spring.

Above from far left: ornately tiled stove in the David Collection; the King's Gardens in winter.

King's Gardens
In their early days, the gardens provided the palace with fish from three fish ponds and fruit and vegetables from orchards and vegetable gardens. Even when the castle became state property in 1849, Rosenborg continued to furnish the royal family with fresh produce until 1909.

Below: the crocus lawn in spring.

Food and Drink 🍴
① ORANGERIET
Kongens Have/Kronprinsessegade 13; tel: 33 11 13 07; Mon–Sat 11.30am–3pm & 6–10pm, Sun noon–4pm; €€€
Opened in 2010, this top-quality pavilion restaurant has views from every window of the King's Garden. Perfect for a glass of wine and immaculate *smørrebrød* on the sunny terrace, or return for a romantic evening meal.

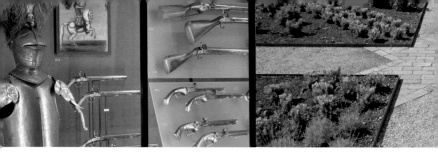

Above from left:
the armory at
Rosenborg Castle;
the herbaceous
border, King's
Garden; royal regalia
in Rosenborg Castle.

No Kids Allowed
When August Saaybe
took the commision
for a sculpture of H.C.
Andersen, he expected
to include children. But
Andersen objected,
saying that he hated
having anyone sitting
or standing close to
him when he read.
He also said that
his fairytales were
intended as much for
adults as for children.

Hans Christian Andersen

With the castle on your left, head on down the Allé. For a civilised coffee break, branch off diagonally for the Orangeriet, see 🍴①. Otherwise continue straight on the **statue of Hans Christian Andersen ⓒ** at its end. This statue was designed and cast during Andersen's lifetime and he had input in to how he was portrayed. It was unveiled in 1880 after Andersen's death. There are some attractive reliefs depicting his stories around the plinth.

Hercules Pavilion and Statue

Turn back and take the first right. Head past a playground and then take the next right to see the **Hercules Pavilion ⓓ** and a modern **statue of Hercules and the Lion ⓔ** performing the first of his 12 Labours: strangling the Nemean Lion with his bare hands in an attempt to atone for a moment of madness and the murder of his three children. The

original marble, bought by Frederik IV in 1708–9 on a trip to Italy, crumbled away: this is a modern copy.

The pavilion (now a café) first known as the 'Blue Arbour', was altered by Christian V so that his family could eat without the servants being present. Beyond the pavilion is the 20th-century **herbaceous border ⓕ**, which is over 250m (820ft) in length and has over 200 plants that change seasonally.

Now head back to the castle, taking a right and then a left through the **Rose Garden ⓖ**, which is laid out in a 16th-century design at the side of the palace. The statue at the end is by the famous sculptor Vilhelm Bissen and depicts Caroline Amalie (1796–1881), wife of Christian VIII, who became queen in 1839. The royal pair were happily married but did not have any children.

ROSENBORG CASTLE

Rosenborg Castle ❸ (Rosenborg Slot; Øster Voldgade 4A; tel: 33 15 32 86; www.rosenborgslot.dk; June–Aug: daily 10am–5pm; May, Sept & Oct: daily 10am–4pm; Jan–Apr & Nov–Dec: Tue–Sun 11am–2pm; charge) is an absolute must-see, bursting with rich detail and unusual objects (such as a joke chair from the 17th century, which squirted its victims with water). However, it is worth buying a guidebook, as there is very little English information inside.

The interior of the castle charts (chronologically) the tastes and needs

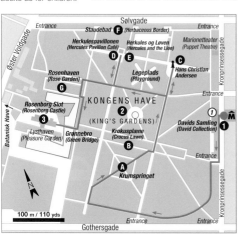

of different kings from Christian IV in the 17th century to Frederik IV, his great-grandson, in the 18th. It was the monarch's primary residence until 1710, when Frederik IV moved out. Since then, it has been used briefly as a residence on two occasions; in 1794 after the fire at Christiansborg and in 1801, when the British bombarded Copenhagen.

On the ground floor, the private **royal apartments**, contain the bedroom in which Christian IV died in 1648 (having been carried from Frederiksborg expressly for the purpose) and a fully tiled, blue-and-white Delft toilet with an embossed ceiling, and the **State Apartments**, including the **Knights' Hall** on the second floor, are packed with solid-silver furniture and countless artefacts alluding to Denmark's success on the world stage.

In the basement, behind massive doors guarded by soldiers, are the Crown Jewels and other exotic royal regalia. The jewels were originally bequeathed for the use of the reigning queen by Queen Sophie Magdalene, 'because', she wrote in her will in 1746, 'in this Royal Family there have been so few jewels, and no Crown Jewels at all'. The Treasury includes other exotic items, such as swords, crowns, a legendary hunting horn, and silver boxes containing the umbilical cords of Frederik III's children.

Before you leave, visit the **Pleasure Garden** on the south side of the palace. It's based on the 17th-century original, in which exotic plants were planted to stand alone for dramatic impact. Exit onto Øster Voldgade at the back of the castle, and turn left. Either cross the road for the entrance to the **Botanical Gardens** or take a short detour down to Gothersgade to visit the **Workers' Museum**.

THE WORKERS' MUSEUM

For the **Workers' Museum ❹** (Arbejdermuseet; Rømersgade 22; tel: 33 93 25 75; www.arbejdermuseet.dk; daily 10am–4pm; charge) take a right on to Gothersgade and a second left on to Rømersgade, where you will find the museum a short way down on the left.

Housed in the former Danish Workers' Movement building, the museum is dedicated to the history of the worker

More Renaissance Splendour
Frederiksborg Slot (tel: 48 26 04 39; www.frederiksborg museet.dk; Apr–Oct daily 10am–5pm; Nov–Mar 11am–3pm; charge) is another superb 17th-century castle built by Christian IV, with a lake and Baroque gardens. Take the S train to Hillerød, 40 mins, and bus 301 or 302 from the station.

History of Rosenborg

First built in 1606 by Christian IV as a summer residence, the palace consisted of the core of the south side of the palace that we know today; two storeys high with a spire-crowned turret facing the city and two bays to the east. In 1611, the central gate tower and drawbridge were added. Further work was done in 1613–15, with an additional two-story wing built on the north side of the gate tower; then another floor (containing the Knights' Hall) was added across the whole building in 1616 along with the spire-crowned towers, and completed in 1624. More work was done ten years later, including an outer double staircase, which was demolished in 1758. The inner staircase, which had connected the first and second floors, was then extended to provide a link with the ground floor.

Botanical Gardens
The first botanical gardens in Copenhagen were founded in 1600. The present ones are the city's fourth and date from 1872.

Below: the elegant Palm House in the Botanical Gardens.

in Denmark. Permanent displays focus on daily life, using models and mannequins to tell each story: a two-room flat belonging to the Sørensen family dates from before World War I; the 1930s flat belongs to the impoverished, out-of-work Petersen family; the prosperity of the 1950s, is seen through the recreation of a coffee shop, shopping street and typical working family's flat; and there's an exhibition on industrial work conditions. The workers' original beer hall is now **Café & Ølhalle 1892**, see ⑪②.

BOTANICAL GARDENS

Return to walk through the **Botanical Gardens** ❺ (Botanisk Have; Øster Farimagsgade 2B; tel: 35 32 22 22; May–Sept: daily 8.30am–6pm, Oct–Mar: Tue–Sun 8.30am–4pm;

free), another lovely green space in the middle of the city, which was given a 17-million-krone facelift in 2010-12.

The Botanical Gardens cover 10 hectares (25 acres) and are home to 25,000 plants belonging to 13,000 species. There are lakes and ponds, pretty bridges, plenty of benches with attractive views, a **Palm House** based on the one at Kew Gardens in Surrey, England, and two small museums, the **Botanical Museum** (Botanisk Museum; open for exhibitions) and the **Geology Museum** (Geologisk Museum; Øster Voldgade 5–7; tel: 35 32 23 45; Tue–Fri 10am–1pm, Sat–Sun 1–4pm; charge).

Repair to the café before heading on to your next port of call, the **National Gallery of Art** *(see p.60)*, and the pretty little Hirschsprung Collection, which stands in its grounds.

HIRSCHSPRUNG
COLLECTION

Exit the gardens onto Sølvgade. Turn right for the National Gallery of Art; otherwise, turn left and then right up Stockholmsgade for the **Hirschsprung Collection ❻** (Hirschsprungske Samling; Stockholmsgade 20; tel: 35 42 03 36; www.hirschsprung.dk; daily 10am–5pm, Wed until 9pm). This charming 100-year-old art gallery (housed in a neoclassical villa designed especially for the collection) stands in the grassy grounds of the Østre Anlæg park, on the site of the old ramparts of Copenhagen.

The paintings and sculptures, which make up an important collection of Danish art from the period known as the 'Golden Age' (1800–50), was gifted to the nation by tobacco tycoon Heinrich Hirschsprung (1836–1908). It is an intimate museum with the art displayed as it might be in a private residence, surrounded by period furniture and artefacts from the artists' homes and studios. Artists featured include those from the Skagen group, the Symbolists and C.W. Eckersberg, who is credited with laying the foundations for the Golden Age.

For lunch, you could try the good, but rather pricey, café in the National Gallery of Art or, better still, make your way to **Aamanns**, see ⑪③.

Above from far left: the lily-pond and exotic flora in the Botanical Gardens.

Food and Drink 🍴

② CAFE & ØLHALLE 1892
Rømersgade 22; tel: 33 33
00 18; 11am–5pm; €
A good selection of Danish food and beer, including 'Stjerne (Star) Pilsner' that still bears the original 1947 label.

③ AAMANNS
10–12 Øster Farimagsgade; tel: 35 55
33 44; deli: Mon–Fri
10.30am–8.30pm, Sat–Sun
noon–4.30pm; restaurant: daily
noon–4pm, Wed–Sat 6–11pm; €€€€€
Fabulous deli offering *smørrebrød* masterpieces. The next door bistro upholds the quality, with its innovative New Nordic dishes.

The Golden Age

The Danish Golden Age spanned the first half of the 19th century and was a time of new ideas and great creativity in the arts. The leading proponents all lived in Copenhagen, then a small city of 10,000 inhabitants, and would have known each other and exchanged ideas. Ironically, as art and culture flourished, Denmark was suffering economically and politically. Important cultural figures at this time were the artist Christofer Eckersberg who introduced a new naturalism and intimacy to painting; C.F. Hansen, the inspired classical architect, who was responsible for rebuilding many of Copenhagen's buildings after the 1795 fire; the great fairytale writer Hans Christian Andersen *(see p.44)*; the philosopher Søren Kirkegaard; the ballet choreographer August Bournonville; and the sculptor Bertel Thorvaldsen.

THE NATIONAL GALLERY OF ART

The Statens Museum for Kunst is Denmark's national art gallery. Housed in a building that reflects two centuries of design, its world-class collection spans 700 years of national and international art.

Bringing Kids
Children are very welcome at the museum; ring ahead or ask at the reception desk about activities on offer. If you have a buggy with you, you must leave it outside, but you can borrow locks and waterproof covers and locks to secure it with from reception. You can then borrow one of the museum's buggies from the entrance hall. Lockers are also available for bags larger than A4 size.

You cannot fail to be impressed by Denmark's **National Gallery of Art** (Statens Museum for Kunst; Sølvgade 48–50; tel: 33 74 84 94; www.smk.dk; Tue, Thur–Sun 10am–5pm, Wed 10am–8pm; free). Its high, airy foyer, winding staircase and view through to the collections beyond are the result of an impressive redesign and the removal of a large central staircase in the 1960s. The collection underwent a dramatic three-year rehang recently, to reflect a more contemporary view of art history.

LEVEL 1

As you walk into the entrance hall, the temporary exhibition spaces are to the left and right. In 2012, exhibitions featured big-hitters Toulouse-Lautrec; Vilhelm Hammerhøi; and Matisse, with loans from Paris and New York. To get your bearings and to explore the mix of old and new architecture, walk through the entrance hall, down the steps to **Sculpture Street ❶**, which runs across the back of the old 19th-century building in a new glass-roofed extension. Here you'll find the latest sculpture exhibitions and large-scale installations (recent works have included, for example, Danish artist FOS's warped buildings, glowing yellow tents and curious machines).

Directly ahead is a set of wide steps, actually the seats of an **amphitheatre ❷**. At the back of its stage is a glass wall, through which you can see the water and greenery of Øster Anlæg, the park at the back of the museum. To the left is a small **children's workshop area ❸** (Sat–Sun 10.30am–4.30pm; charge), where professional artists help kids to explore their creativity; enter via the stairs on Sculpture Street. Nearby is the **x-rummet ❹**, containing works commissioned by contemporary artists especially for this unusual space.

LEVEL 2

The second level is home to the collections. Take the lift in the main entrance hall to Level 2, to the landing opposite Room 201.

European Art 1300-1800

Room 201A contains an overview of the gallery's impressive collection of European art ❺, which includes works by Titian, El Greco and Rubens. Particularly intriguing in this room is Lucas Cranach the Elder's oil-on-wood *Melancholy* (1532), an allegorical work in which an angel apparently rues man's predilection for violence.

Three routes wend their way chronologically through the European section, tracing artists from Italy, the Netherlands and Northern Europe. The Italian route begins around the corner in **Room 201B** with examples of Renaissance and Gothic art, including the glowering marble sculpture *Head of a Bearded Man* (1312) by Giovanni Pisano and the lovely *Meeting of St Anne and St Joachim at the Golden Gate* by Filipino Lippi (1457–1504), plus two handsome El Greco portraits and a Titian. Seventeenth-century artworks include Salvator Rosa's emotionally-charged *Diogenes Throwing Away his Drinking Cup* (1651), black with

Above from far left: the original building dates back to 1896; the interior of the museum has been redeveloped to allow for exhibits to be displayed with better lighting and space; sculpture in the museum gardens.

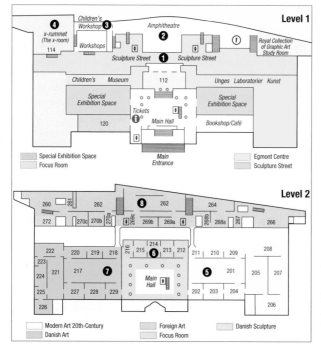

Collection History
The original collection, once the private collection of the king, first went on show to the public in 1822 at Christiansborg Palace. Fortunately, it escaped the palace fire in 1884 and the National Gallery of Art, designed by Vilhelm Dahlerup, was opened in 1886. The gallery's extension dates from 1998.

stormclouds. In **Room 201E** internal torment gives way to an 18th-century interest in Italian travel and land- and city-scapes, with some beautiful paintings by Tiepolo and Guardi.

Route 2, looking at art from the Netherlands, threads through a suite of small rooms (211B to 209) holding works by Thomas de Keyser, Willem Kolf and Adrien de Vries, a Dutch Mannerist sculptor; and in **Room 209**, works from Rembrandt's workshop.

Route 3 covers the rest of Northern Europe. It begins with a question – what does it mean to be a 'good man'? – and answers it in **Rooms 202 and 203** with works including an altar panel by Petrus Christus dating from 1450; Cranach's famous *Portrait of Martin Luther* (the two were friends), dating from the height of the Reformation; the comic but faintly unsettling *Strife of Lent with Shrovetide* by Bruegel the Elder; and Cornelis de Vos's *Judgement Day*. **Room 204** is dedicated to Rubens (1577–1640), with portraits of *Francesco de' Medici* and *Joanna of Austria*, and Rubens' masterpiece, *The Judgement of Solomon* (1617).

Cross Room 205 and enter **Room 206**, containing examples of painstaking and detailed *trompe l'oeil*. **Rooms 207** and **208A** nod to the Danes' 17th- and 18th-century love of all things French, with work by Nattier and Fragonard amongst others, and lead you round again to **Room 205**, where you can check out the delicacy of the butterfly placement in Cornelisz van Haarlem's *Fall of the Titans* (1599–90).

French Art 1900–30
Retrace your steps to the landing above the foyer, where **Rooms 212–216** ❻ contain a real treat: pieces by international artists who were part of the early 20th-century Parisian art scene. Highlights include several works by Matisse (1869–1954) in **Room 214**, including the famous *Portrait of Madame Matisse* (1905), also known as *The Green Line*, which gave rise to the name of the French splinter art group, The Fauves (or 'wild animals'), whose work was characterised by a strong use of intuitive colour. The Matisses were gathered by a far-sighted engineer, Johannes Rump, who donated them in 1928. The gallery also owns 147 paintings, sculptures and ceramics by Picasso, some of which are on display in **Room 213**, along with a prize Modigliani, *Alice* (1918). The *embarras de richesses* doesn't stop there: other great artists include Dufy (**Room 212**); Braque and Gris (**Room 213**); Derain (**Room 215**); and Léger (**Room 216**).

Danish & Nordic Art 1750–1900
Back on the landing, turn right into **Rooms 217–29** ❼, a section dedicated to Danish and Nordic art that includes the period 1800–50, an era known as the Golden Age (see p.59) in which the arts flourished, new ideas and styles came to the fore, and, in the arts, a turning to nature and the everyday condition of the world and its inhabitants was paramount. **Room 217**, divided into six sections, gives an overview, which continues in **Rooms 218–20** (turn right as you leave 217F). C.W. Eckersberg, a

Golden-Age giant, is well represented with *Bella and Hanna* (1820); *A View through Three of the Colosseum's North-Western Arches* (1815); and *Russian Ship of the Line 'Asow'* (1828).

Other rooms in this section are themed. **Room 221** – 'The Body in Art' – includes the rather ominous *Lady in Black* (1892) by the angst-ridden Edvard Munch; and Ejnar Nielsen's raw and mesmerising *And in his Eyes I saw Death* (1897), in which a hollow-eyed figure looking like a young Omar Sharif waits by a coffin, staring hopelessly at the future that awaits him. **Rooms 223–224** explore the emergence of modern-day Denmark: highlights include Anna Ancher's *A Funeral* (1891); Michael Ancher's *A Lifeboat is Taken Through the Dunes*; Theodor Philipsen's *Late Autumn Day in the Jægersborg Deer Park*; and works by P.S. Krøyer; all of whom were strongly influenced by French Impressionism.

Room 228 is dedicated to Vilhelm Hammershøi's trademark grey works (washed-out interiors, muted portraits and ghostly paintings of Copenhagen's buildings), and features Portrait of Ida Ilsted (1890), recently saved for the nation thanks to a large donation from the charitable foundation Augustinus Fonden. Imbued with light and cheer, **Room 229** – 'Willumsen and Vitalism' – contains Johannes Larsen's sun-splashed *Children Playing, Enghave Square* (1908) and J.F. Willumsen's *Mountain Climber* (1912), a statuesque woman in perfect harmony with the landscape.

Danish & International Art from 1900

From the landing, cross a bridge over Sculpture Street to **Rooms 260–272 ⑧**, which are dedicated to modern art. This section underwent a complete rehang in 2012, with the final displays still to be chosen at the time of writing. Expect great things: the museum's modern collection contains some particularly fine pieces, especially by the CoBrA group, a collective of post-war avant-garde artists from Copenhagen, Brussels and Amsterdam. Their colourful works tended towards the surreal, with an abstract distortion of images often borrowed from primitive and folk art. Carl-Henning Pedersen, known as the 'Scandinavian Chagall', was a founder member: his paintings are filled with

Above from far left:
Melancholy, by Lucas Cranach the Elder; *Still Life with Door, Guitar and Bottles,* by Pablo Picasso.

Below: Portrait of Madame Matisse, The Green Line (1905) by Henri Matisse.

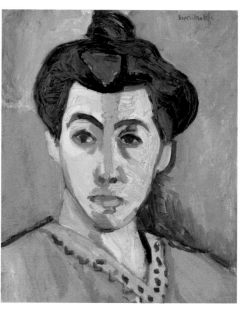

Above from left:
J.F. Willumsen's
A Mountain Climber
(detail; 1912); Per
Kirkeby's *Untitled*
(detail; 1995); along
the reservoirs.

Above: *The Negress*
by Cubist sculptor
Henri Laurens (1934).

Below: the
contemporary works.

cosmic imagery, dominated by abstract, otherworldly birds. Just before his death in 2007, Pedersen donated 40 works to the gallery. Among his most famous are *Humans and Animals in the Landscape* (1942), *The Turkish Drum* (1960) and *Out Into the Wide World* (1988).

Even better known is fellow CoBrA founder Asger Jorn, a political radical and prolific artist who produced some 2,500 paintings, sculptures, prints and tapestries during his lifetime, as well as fomenting rebellion against the 'established' art world. Works include *Orange Object* (1944) and his almost fairytale-like *Wheel of Life* (1953), a universal and timeless theme that he took up after recovering from tuberculosis in 1951.

Installations of the love-'em-or-hate-'em kind, such as subversive creations by Danish/Norwegian collaborators Michael Elmgreen and Ingar Dragset, are set to surprise in this section: their

eerie *Please, Keep Quiet* (2003) unnerved visitors with its detailed reconstruction of a hospital ward.

Bjørn Nørgaard (b.1947), a prominent member of the current Danish art scene, is well represented in the gallery's collection. Daring and challenging works include the iconic photo series *The Female Christ* (1969) and the 17-minute film *Horse Sacrifice* (1970), which both caused a huge furore in their day. Over time, Nørgaard has become a royal favourite, designing 11 tapestries for Christiansborg Palace as well as Queen Margrethe's sarcophagus *(see p.90)*.

The gallery also holds more than 700 pieces by another of Denmark's greats, Per Kirkeby (b.1938), who has spent more than four decades exploring broad metaphysical concepts. Landscape and nature are recurring themes, depicted with characteristically vigorous, thickly-textured brushstrokes. In commenting on his thought processes as he paints, Kirkeby rather comfortably says that if he makes a mistake, 'it doesn't matter much; I can always paint over it'. It's now time to have a rest and digest all the artwork that you have seen with a visit to the café on Level 1, see ⑪①.

Food and Drink

① CAFÉEN
Level 1; tel: 33 74 84 94; Tue–Sun
4.50pm, Wed 10am–7.50pm; €–€€
Lovely fresh food, all cooked on the
spot and served in stylish surroundings, designed by artists Bjørn
Nørgaard and Peter Lassen, with
great views.

NØRREBRO AND ALONG THE RESERVOIRS

The main things to do in Nørrebro are walking in the cemetery on a nice day and meandering around the shopping streets around Sankt Hans Torv. Weather-permitting, the reservoirs are a pleasant spot for a walk or jog.

Nørrebro (North Bridge) lies beyond the reservoirs. It started off as a staunch working-class district in the 19th century. It still has a reputation for political activism, and is a lively, multi-cultural place to hang out or shop.

Start on the city side of **Dronning Louises Bro ❶** (Bridge), a popular gathering point for public demonstrations. On your left is **Peblinge Sø** (lake), while on your right is **Sortedams Sø**.

Walk down Nørrebrogade and turn left on Blågårdsgade passing through **Blågårds Plads ❷**. This avenue once lead to Blågård mansion, named for its distinctive blue roof tiles, which burnt down in 1835. On your left, note the 22 granite statues along the edges of the sunken square (where a few beer drinkers may be hanging out). They were carved on site by sculptor Kai Nielsen who used the locals as his inspiration. Cross the square and turn right up Korsgade as far as Kapelvej. Turn right at Helligkors Kirke, following the street around until you reach the entrance to the cemetery on your left.

ASSISTENS KIRKEGARD

This **churchyard ❸** (Apr–Sept: 7am–10pm, Oct–Mar: 7am–7pm; free) is

DISTANCE 4.5km (2¾ miles)
TIME A half day
START Drønnings Louise Bro
END Tycho Brahe Planetarium
POINTS TO NOTE
It's a long walk from the centre: bus 5A from Rådhuspladsen to Dronning Louises Brø will shorten the journey.

very popular with the locals, especially in summer, when you will see plenty of joggers, sunbathers and mothers with buggies. It was laid out in 1760 to relieve pressure on the city graveyards, which were full to overflowing after several outbreaks of plague had killed over one third of the population (23,000 people) in just 50 years. For a map and list of famous graves, including H.C. Andersen, Søren Kierkegaard, Niels Bohr and Dan Turréll, turn right at the entrance. For Hans Christian Andersen *(see p.44)*, turn left.

Come out of the same gate, walk left along Kappelvej, then turn right onto Nørrebrogade. Cross the road and walk down to **Elmegade ❹**, a popular shopping street. Browse in the likes of Goggle, Fünf and Elektrocute for streetwise clothing and accessories. For a

Above: the Tycho Brahe Planetarium cuts a striking figure behind the reservoirs.

Start at Either End
You can start this walk in Nørrebro and walk back to the inner city taking in the Tycho Brahe Planetarium, or you can start at the Planetarium and spend the afternoon/evening in Nørrebro. Either way, stop for a drink to take in the local atmosphere.

Above from left:
laundry and lattes at
the Laundromat Café;
the solar system in
the Planetarium; leafy
Fredericksberg;
outdoor ice-skating.

coffee or a bite to eat, drop into the
Laundromat Café, see ⑪①, or keep on
until you reach **Sankt Hans Torv** ❺,
the central place to hang out in summer.
Here, **Pussy Galore's Flying Circus**, see
⑪②, is popular.

Cross the square and walk down
Sankt Hans Gade. At the first junc-

tion, you can either continue on to
Café 22, see ⑪③. or turn right on to
Ravnsborggade ❻, which is full of
bric-a-brac and antique shops. At the
end, turn left onto Nørrebrogade. Just
before Dronning Louises Bro, turn
right down **Peblinge Dossering** ❼,
stopping to enjoy the view from one of
many reservoir-side benches.

Continue alongside the water to the
Tycho Brahe Planetarium ❽
(Gammel Kongevej 10; tel: 33 12 12 24;
Mon 11.30am–8.30pm, Tue–Thur
9.30am–8.30pm, Fri–Sun 10.30am–
8.30pm; charge), which has some interesting displays and an IMAX cinema.

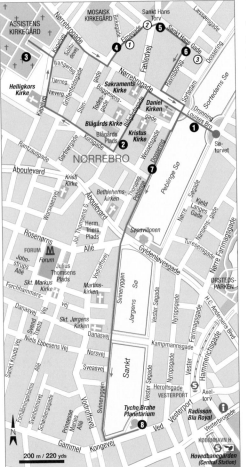

FREDERIKSBERG

Leafy Frederiksberg is Copenhagen's upmarket – formerly royal – suburb, and home to Frederiksberg Slot, Søndermarken and the underground Glass Museum, the zoo and attractive, tree-lined, residential boulevards. Although so close to the centre, it is a municipality independent of Copenhagen.

Until the 18th century, Frederiksberg was a small country village. It rose to prominence as the concept of a country retreat began to appeal to middle-class and wealthy town dwellers. These included Frederik IV who, inspired by his travels in Italy, built a summer palace in the grounds of a former royal farm at the end of Frederiksberg Allé.

This walk starts at **Frederiksberg Runddel ❶**, in front of the park gates. Every winter (Nov–Mar), there is an outdoor skating rink here. This is not far from the junction of Vesterbrogade and **Frederiksberg Allé**, formerly the rather grand private road that led to the castle. When you walk along this major boulevard you will pass several theatres, a war memorial and **Frederiksberg Chokolade**, an excellent chocolate shop, see ⑪①. As you approach the *runddel* (square), you will pass a cemetery on your left belonging to **Frederiksberg Church**. To visit the church, turn left onto Pile Allé.

FREDERIKSBERG CHURCH

Frederiksberg Church ❷ (Frederiksberg Kirke; Frederiksberg Allé 65; daily 8am–5pm), with its pyramidal roof, was built in the Baroque style by

DISTANCE 2km (1¼ miles)
TIME A full day
START Frederiksberg Runddel
END Memorial Mound
POINTS TO NOTE

This walk works well in both directions – in summer the zoo is open late, so it makes sense to go there last; in winter you may want to go there first. You can also tack this walk, or part of it, onto the Vesterbro walk (see p.26–31). Turn right at the top of Ny Carlsberg Vej, cross the road and up some steps into Søndermarken. Follow the path to Frederiksberg Castle and the zoo.

architect Felix Dusart in 1732–34 and is notable for its octagonal shape, the first of its kind in Denmark. Inside,

Food and Drink

① FREDERIKSBERG CHOKOLADE
Frederiksberg Allé 64; tel: 33 22 36 35; Mon–Thur 10am–5.30pm, Fri 10am–6pm, Sat 10am–2pm; €€
Exquisite handmade cakes and chocolates. Highlights include realistic-looking chocolate flowers – or how about a chocolate chess set? Also runs courses, if you want to learn their secrets.

Get Lost
You'll find an unusual beech-hedge maze on Pile Allé, just next to De Små Haver – it's laid out in the shape of a Tuborg beer-bottle label. In spite of its alcoholic origins, it's a good place for kids to play hide-and-seek.

Above from left:
Frederiksberg Gardens are home to many species of birds; Frederiksberg Castle; a Chinese bridge.

there are four attractive, green-painted wooden galleries, which were added in 1864. Many important Danes are buried in the graveyard, including figures from the Danish 'Golden Age' *(see p.59)*, such as the poet Adam Oehlenschläger *(see p.31)* and his children.

ALLÉGADE

Before entering the park opposite, turn right and walk up **Allégade ❸**, a pretty street lined with restaurants and cafés set back from the road. This is one of Frederiksberg's oldest streets, dating from the 1650s when the first farmers settled here. Since the end of the 18th century, it has also been the place to have fun and in 1784, there were 34 pubs ranged along here. **Allégade 10** on your right dates from this period.

On your left, as you walk up, there is also the **Museum of Danish Revue Theatre ❹** (Revymuseet; Allégade 5;

tel: 38 10 20 45; Tue–Sun 11am–4pm; charge), a celebration of Danish music-hall and variety acts that may be lost on non-Danes.

STORM P MUSEUM

Return to Frederiksberg Runddel, where you will find the main entrance to the park. On the left is a delightful small museum, the **Storm P Museum ❺** (Storm P Museet; Frederiksberg Runddel; tel: 38 86 05 23; May–Sept: Tue–Sun 10am– 4pm, Oct–Mar: Wed, Sat, Sun 10am–4pm; charge), which is dedicated to Storm P.

This witty Danish cartoonist's work seems to combine the social realism of the late 19th and early 20th centuries with the ludicrous inventions of Heath Robinson and some of the cartoon qualities of Mr Magoo. Marvellous if you understand Danish, but still worth popping in for the visual style and humour even if you do not.

The Dummy Tree
Generations of Danish children have consigned their last dummy (pacifier) to the branches of the Dummy Tree in Frederiksberg Gardens.

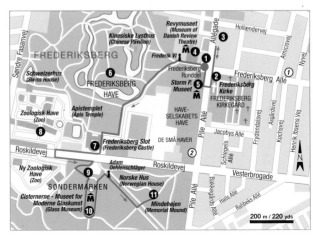

FREDERIKSBERG GARDENS

If lunch or supper is looming, visit one of the three small, very traditional Danish restaurants called 'De Små Haver' (The Small Gardens), next to the Frederiksberg Gardens (Frederiksberg Have), before you go any further: **Hansens Gamle Familiehave**, see ⑪②, is open all year-round.

Enter the **park ❻** through the main gate (open daily from 7am; closing times vary from 10pm May–Aug to 5pm Jan; free). In the 19th century, there used to be a guard here charged with keeping out anyone he considered undesirable (including seamen and people with dogs).

Just inside the gates there is a **statue of King Frederik VI** (1808–39) by H.W. Bissen. Frederik VI, cousin to Britain's king, George VI, governed as Regent from 1784 and was responsible for abolishing serfdom in 1788. He was also Regent during the British attacks on Copenhagen in 1801 and 1807. The inscription on the plinth translates as, 'Here he felt happy in the midst of loyal people'.

There is a park map at the entrance. To the right, you will find yourself walking (or better still, rowing – boats can be hired from May to September) around the meandering canal system within the park. Turn left and walk along the side of the park for the quickest route to Frederiksberg Castle and the zoo.

The park was originally a formal Baroque garden but in 1798–1804 was remodelled in the fashionable English 'Romantic' style, complete with picturesque follies. These include the **Chinese pavilion** (May–Aug: Sun 2–4pm; free; cross by the ferry boat); the **Møstings House**, a listed, pretty neoclassical house; the **Swiss House**, a little cottage built for the royal family to take tea; and the colonnaded **Apis Temple**. A colony of grey herons nests close to the Chinese pavilion. The males arrive in March and the females in May – they can often be seen wandering the lawns and paths.

Frederiksberg Castle ❼ (Frederiksberg Slot; closed to the public), standing at the south end of the gardens, is now a military academy. Walk up to its terrace and admire the view along the broad axis that is part of the original Baroque design. In the 19th century, you could see as far as the Sound from here.

Leave via the exit on the other side of the castle and turn right, walking down Roskildevej until you reach the zoo. The park opposite is **Søndermarken**, and the far end of Vesterbro *(see p.26)* lies on the other side.

Above: the Chinese pavilion where, in the 19th century, Frederik VI took afternoon tea with his family; Frederiksberg Gardens are an oasis of tranquillity.

Food and Drink 🍴

② HANSENS GAMLE FAMILIEHAVE

Pile Allé 16; tel: 36 30 92 57; www.hansenshave.dk; Mon–Sat 11am–midnight, Sun 11am–6pm; closed Mon–Tue in Jan & Feb; €–€€
This cosily old-fashioned place – with its checked tablecloths, twinkly lights and traditional Danish smørrebrød – dates back to 1850, when it sold boiling water to park visitors to make do-it-yourself coffee.

Above from left: lions and zebra at the zoo; the Ny Carlsberg Glyptotek; mother and child in the Glyptotek's Winter Garden.

Above: the zoo also hosts elephants (in their designer enclosure), baboons, prairie dogs and brown bears (*right*).

Famous Danes

The Glass Museum contains art works created by some of Denmark's most famous modern artists including, Per Kirkeby, Carl Henning Pedersen, Bjørn Nørgaard and Robert Jacobsen.

THE ZOO

The **zoo** ❽ (Roskildevej 32; www.zoo. dk; tel: 72 20 02 00; July: 10am–9pm; June–Aug: 10am–6pm; Apr, May, Sept–Oct: 10am–5pm; Jan–Mar & Nov–Dec: 10am–4pm; charge) is not just of interest to children, especially on a sunny summer evening. As zoos go, it is an excellent one, with lots on offer, including elephants in an enclosure designed by Norman Foster, tigers, brown bears, polar bears and a marvellous pride of lions. There is a viewing tower, and a café close to the entrance.

SØNDERMARKEN

Opposite the zoo is another garden **Søndermarken** ❾ (daily 24 hours; free). The **Glass Museum** is in sight of the road (the entrance is inside one of the two glass pyramids), and the **Memorial Mound** is down a path to your left.

Glass Museum
The **Glass Museum** ❿ (Cisternerne – Museet for Moderne Glaskunst; weekends and public hols 11am–5pm; also Mar–Oct: Thur–Fri 2pm–6pm, Nov and Feb Thur–Fri 2pm–5pm; charge) is worth a visit for its location alone. Housed in an underground water tank built after the cholera epidemic of 1853, its arches stretch out in all directions like a crypt, water occasionally drips gently from the ceiling, lifesize limestone statues loom out of the darkness at you and richly decorated modern stained-glass works glow

in the gloom. It's an atmospheric, almost medieval, experience that you are unlikely to find anywhere else.

Memorial Mound
Walk back towards the castle and turn right. You will pass a **statue of the poet Adam Oehlenschläger**, who ran around the park as a child because his father was the Palace Steward, and the **Norwegian House**, a romantic folly dating from 1787, before reaching the **mound ⓫** (open 4 July only) on your left. It is surrounded by tall trees and commemorates Denmark's emigrants. The words above the entrance translate, 'They who set out, never to return'. Inside, at the end of a stone passage, there is a cavern, a cupola letting in light above the life-size figure of a woman representing Mother Denmark, who is embracing her children.

The easiest way to get back to the centre of town is on the No. 6A bus from outside the zoo.

MUSEUMS AND PLEASURE GARDENS

For a lovely day and evening of culture and fun, this is an excellent circular walk, taking in up to three art galleries and museums during the day and Tivoli, Copenhagen's historic pleasure gardens, in the evening.

NY CARLSBERG GLYPTOTEK

This tour begins on the steps of the **Ny Carlsberg Glyptotek** ❶ (Dantes Plads 7; tel: 33 41 81 41; www.glyp toteket.dk; Tue–Sun 11am–5pm; charge except Sun), a wonderful art gallery housing the collections of Carl Jacobsen (1842–1914), son of the founder of Carlsberg beer. His taste was predominantly for the ancient and classical and with his wife Ottilia, he built up one of the world's best collections of Egyptian, Greek, Roman and Etruscan art. Much of the world-class modern collection showcasing the Impressionists, Post-Impressionists and Danish 19th-century art was built up after his death.

Level 1

As you pass through the impressive porticoed facade, you can see through

DISTANCE 1.5km (1 mile)
TIME A full day
START Ny Carlsberg Glyptotek
END Tivoli
POINTS TO NOTE
It's easy to spend a day in the Glyptotek so keep an eye on the time if you want to visit the other museums as well.

to the grand, airy 19th-century **Winter Garden**, strewn with plants and statues and home to the museum's excellent café, see ⑪①. Directly ahead are the steps to level 2; at the far end on the left is the entrance to the modern extension.

Level 2

Level 2 is home to the **Greek and Roman Collections**, the **Egyptian collection** and **19th-century French and Danish sculpture**. Among many other treasures, including a whole room dedicated to **Rodin**, this is the place to come for an intimate picture of the faces of the past, including such notaries as Alexander the Great, his father Philip of Macedonia, the Roman emperors Caligula (still with traces of ancient paint on the face), Augustus

A 'Glyptotek'
For Carl Jacobsen, sculpture was the most important art form and the word 'glyptotek' means 'a collection of statues'.

Food and Drink 🍴

① CAFE GLYPTOTEK
Tel: 33 41 81 28; Tue–Sun 11am–4.45pm; €–€€
Lovely salads and light lunch dishes but especially popular for its home-made cakes.

Above from left:
designer chairs in the Dansk Design Center; the Greek and Roman collection at the Glyptotek; ethnic masks at the National Museum.

Gift to the Nation
Carl Jacobsen gave his collection to the nation in 1888 on the understanding that the state build a suitable building for it. When the first part was opened in 1897, it lay in open country with a view to the east across the swampy environs of the harbour. Jacobsen thought it rather remote and inappropriately close to plebeian Tivoli.

and Hadrian. Don't miss the atmospheric Egyptian collection, which you enter down steps as if in to a tomb. Among the startling collection of artefacts are some wonderful sarcophagi plus painted models of tombs and scenes of Egyptian daily life.

The Modern Wing
The modern wing, designed by the architect Henning Larsen, houses a beautiful collection of **Etruscan and Mediterranean art** and an impressive **French collection**, which includes works by artists such as Gauguin, Degas, Monet, Manet, Bonnard, Van Gogh, Cézanne, Renoir, Pissarro and Berthe Morisot. Look out for Degas' statue of a 14-year-old dancer, Manet's *Absinthe Drinker* (1859), Van Gogh's *Landscape from St Rémy* (1889) and Gauguin's *Skaters in Frederiksberg Gardens* (1884), dating from the time

(1883–4) that he and his Danish wife and family lived in Copenhagen.

DANSK DESIGN CENTER

Cross the road and visit the **Dansk Design Center** ❷ (H.C. Andersens Boulevard 27–9; tel: 33 69 33 69; www.ddc.dk; Mon–Tue and Thur–Fri 10am–5pm, Wed 10am–9pm, Sat–Sun 11am–4pm; charge) for one of their exhibitions on cutting-edge design. The striking building is the work of architect Lars Henning. There's also another good café here, the **Café Dansk**, see ⑪②.

NATIONAL MUSEUM

The next port of call is the **National Museum** ❸ (National Museet; Ny Vestergade 10; tel: 33 13 44 11; www.natmus.dk; Tue–Sun 10am–5pm; free

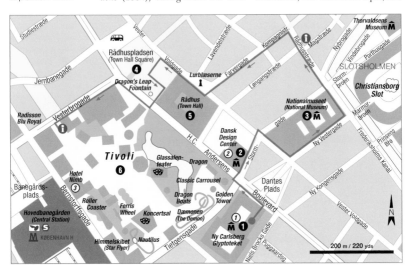

guided tours June–Sept: Tue, Thur & Sun 11am; free), Denmark's national cultural collection. Walk down Stormgade, take a right on Vester Voldgade and first left down Ny Vestergade. The museum is a little way down on the left.

The collection ranges from the prehistoric period to the modern day in Denmark and also includes a wonderful ethnographic collection. The ground floor is home to prehistory and the children's museum. The first to third floors can be confusing but the rooms all run around the atrium with ethnography, coins and medals, the Middle Ages and the state rooms on the first floor; the history of Denmark (1660–2000) and more ethnographic collections (including those of the Inuit) on the second floor; and Near Eastern and Greek and Roman antiquities on the third floor.

Ground Floor

The museum's amazing **prehistoric exhibition** includes unique archaeological treasures such as the **Gundestrup Cauldron**, thought to show scenes of human sacrifice and one of the world's few depictions of the Iron-age god Cernunnos; the **Trundholm Chariot of the Sun**, dating from *c*.1200 BC, when the Danes worshipped the sun, imagining it riding through the sky in a chariot pulled by a celestial horse; and the fascinating **Egtved grave** belonging to a blonde young woman wearing a string skirt, bodice, dagger and hairnet. A companion grave belongs to a young man with a full head of hair and rings in his ears.

First Floor

As you come up the stairs from the atrium, facing towards the street, the **Danish Middle Ages and Renaissance** is located on your left and an **ethnographic collection** on the right.

The two collections are, in many ways, similar; both vast, both charting the social and religious practices of a time and place, from minute articles to entire rooms and houses. (Both collections also continue directly above on the second floor.) Don't miss the **Royal Apartments** (Rooms 127–134), including the marvellous **Great Hall**, which date from the 1740s when the building was still a royal palace, home to the Crown Prince Frederik V.

The ethnographic collection on this floor includes artefacts from **Africa**, **India**, **Indonesia**, **New Guinea**, **New Zealand**, **Japan**, **China**, **Central Asia** and **Siberia** as well as a **music room** featuring world music and a fascinating slide presentation.

RÅDHUSPLADSEN

From the National Museum, turn left. At the bottom of Ny Vestergade you'll

Tiniest and Oldest
The museum's tiniest exhibit is a shoe carved from a cherry pip. It is part of the original royal collection. You can also see Denmark's oldest coin, minted at the behest of Sweyn Forkbeard, Harald Bluetooth's son, about 1,000 years ago.

Tivoli Ride Tickets
To go on any of the rides you need to either buy a multi-ride pass (3–11s 160dkk; over-12s 200dkk), which lasts all day, or separate tickets (10dkk); rides need two–six tickets each. If you have a Copenhagen card (see p.107) and just wish to wander, this will let you in for free.

Below: the Lurblæserne stand tall on Rådhuspladsen.

find the Frederiksholms Kanal and the island of Slotsholmen (see p.76). For Rådhuspladsen turn left again and third left onto Farvergade Kompagnistraede, home to the astronomer Tycho Brahe in 1597, until you come to **Rådhuspladsen ❹**.

The square, which dates from the end of the 19th century, is now a large space surrounded by hotels and restaurants. The current construction works, due to continue until 2017, mark the building of a new metro station.

Rådhuspladsen plays an active part in city life and is the site for Christmas and New Year festivities and concerts. It is dominated by the town hall or Rådhus, dating from 1905 after the town hall

on Nytorv (see p.33) became too small for the city's needs. In front of it is the **Dragon's Leap Fountain**, likened to a spittoon at its unveiling in 1904: the addition of the dramatic bull in 1923 silenced the critics. Next to it the **Lurblæserne**, two bronze lur-blowers atop a 12m (40ft) brick column; local lore has it that the horns sound if a virgin walks past! Originally only one horn-player was planned for the monument, which explains the men's jostle for space.

Town Hall

The **Town Hall ❺** (Rådhus; Rådhuspladsen 1; tel: 33 66 25 83; Mon–Fri 8am–5pm, Sat 9.30am–1pm; free; tours in English Mon–Fri 3pm, Sat 10am) was built in mock-Gothic style by architect Martin Nyrop in 1905. A statue of Bishop Absalon and fantastical sea creatures adorn the faade. Inside, the entrance hall is a flurry of pseudo-Renaissance splendour with golden mosaics and a minstrels' gallery. Visitors can climb the 300 steps up the splendid **clock tower** (entry by tour only, Mon–Fri 11am & 2pm, Sat noon; charge) for an excellent view of the city and also see **Jens Olsens Verdensur** (Mon–Fri 8.30am–4.30pm, Sat 10am–1pm; charge), which, according to *Guinness World Records*, is the world's most accurate clock and is said to have over 14,000 parts. If it is sunny or you just need a place to sit down, there is a pretty **garden** (daily 10am–4pm) with benches behind the Town Hall. Walk down either side of the building and walk through the first open gateway that you reach.

Food and Drink 🍴

③ HERMAN
Tivoli; tel: 88 70 00 20; www.restaurantherman.dk; Mon–Fri noon–1.30pm, Mon–Sat 6–9.30pm; €€€–€€€€
A real Danish gastronomic treat. Delicious food served in a classic dining room, given a romantic tint by Tivoli's dancing coloured lights.

TIVOLI

To visit **Tivoli** ❻ (Vesterbrogade 3; tel: 33 15 10 01; ticket booking: 33 15 10 12; www.tivoli.dk; mid-Apr–late Sept: daily 11am–late, mid-Oct: daily 11am–11pm; mid-Nov–Dec: Sun–Thur 11am–10pm, Fri–Sat 11am–11pm; charge), cross H.C. Andersens Boulevard by the writer's statue to the entrance opposite.

Founded in 1843 outside the city walls, Tivoli is as popular now as it has ever been with over five million visitors every year. Ignore the cynics, this is a great day or night out whether you go on the rides or not. There are plenty of rides for adults and kids alike – the former rather more stomach-churning and scream-inducing than the latter. For the hardy, there are four roller coasters: **Dæmonen** is the most extreme, looping the loop at speeds of up to 80kmh (50mph). **Himmelskibet**, the tallest carrousel in the world at 80m (260ft) high, also gets its riders' hearts pumping. The **dragon boats** on the lake, the **pantomime theatre**, the **Tivoli boys guard**, trees and lakes all lit with Chinese lanterns have a romantic appeal for non-adrenalin junkies.

There is also lots of music and drama here: the **concert hall** is one of the best in Copenhagen offering ballet and opera (buy tickets in advance); the **open-air stage** sees loud, free rock and pop concerts every Friday night; and the pantomime theatre is free, as are the many musical groups playing on bandstands throughout the park.

If you get peckish, there are over 40 eateries ranging from juice stalls to top-end restaurants, including the Michelin-starred **Herman**, see ⑪③. Alternatively, bring a sandwich, sit on a bench and people-watch.

Above from far left: the bright lights of Tivoli; the Town Hall far and close-up; up, up and away in Tivoli.

Tivoli – i lov iT
There are plenty of rides for the kids, including a Viking-ship merry-go-round, flying aeroplanes, miniature classic cars, an old-fashioned trolley bus ride and a traditional carrousel. The newest ride is the Nautilus, spins its victims through 360° at a stomach-lurching 160kmh (100mph).

Left: Tivoli is a collage of architectural styles that includes Chinese pagodas, Moorish palaces and everything in between.

SLOTSHOLMEN

Slotsholmen is the oldest site in Copenhagen for it was here, in 1167, that Bishop Absalon built a castle to protect the little fishing village of Havn from the unwanted advances of German pirates. A castle has stood here ever since and, 900 years later, the island is still the centre of national government.

DISTANCE 2km (1¼ miles)
TIME A full day
START Palace forecourt
END Black Diamond
POINTS TO NOTE

This route is not the most leisurely, packing in lot of sights, especially if you stop for lunch. It's a great day for busy sightseeing, though.

This is the fifth castle to stand on Slotsholmen (Castle Island). The first was a fortress surrounded by a limestone wall; it lasted 200 years before it was destroyed in 1367 by the Hanseatic League, a German alliance of trading guilds that monopolised trade in the Baltic and Northern Europe.

The second castle was built in 1375; in 1417 it gained in importance when the Danish king, Erik of Pomerania,

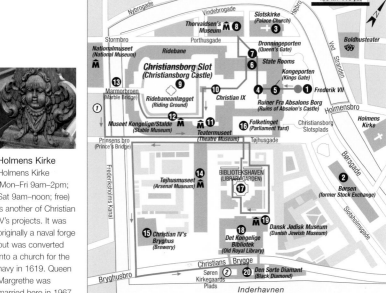

Holmens Kirke
Holmens Kirke (Mon–Fri 9am–2pm; Sat 9am–noon; free) is another of Christian IV's projects. It was originally a naval forge but was converted into a church for the navy in 1619. Queen Margrethe was married here in 1967.

made Kjøbmandehavn (now Merchants' Havn, reflecting its growing commercial success) his state capital. It was enlarged over the years but by the 18th century was falling down – something commented upon by visiting dignitaries – and Christian VI, mindful of his position razed it to the ground.

The third castle, a beautiful Baroque palace, was erected between 1731 and 1745 but it fell victim to fire in 1794 and only the magnificent stables and intimate red-and-gold theatre escaped the flames *(see p.79)*. Homeless, the royal family repaired to the mansions of the aristocratic elite at Amalienborg from which they never returned *(see p.47)*.

Between 1803 and 1828 a fourth castle, designed by the classical architect C.F. Hansen, was built. Used for ceremonial occasions and entertaining, in 1848 it, too, went up in smoke, with just the Palace Church and the Riding Ground left standing.

The fifth and current castle was built between 1907 and 1928 by Thorvald Jørgensen who, mindful of the fate of its predecessors, built its walls of reinforced concrete with granite facings. It is home to the State Rooms, the Folketinget (Parliament), Prime Minister's Office and Supreme Court.

SLOTSHOLMEN IN A DAY

Before you enter the castle through the main gate, facing Holmens Kirke *(see margin, p.76)*, take a look in the forecourt at the **equestrian statue ❶** by H.W. Bissen, which represents Frederik VII (1848–63). Note, too, the

building on your left with the twisted spire. This is the **Stock Exchange ❷**, (Børsen; closed to the public but you can take a virtual tour at http://english. borsbygningen.dk), built in 1618–24 by Christian IV, who wanted to make Copenhagen a great trading centre *(see p.82)*. The building was constructed with many doors on a narrow dam with water on both sides, so that goods could be unloaded directly into the building from ships. It originally housed a simple hall, which had storage space on the ground floor and booths and offices on the upper floor. In 1625, Christian enhanced the building by adding 18 gables and a 54m (177ft) spire, made up of four entwined dragons' tails, said to protect the building. The three golden crowns on top represent Denmark, Norway and Sweden.

It did not become a stock exchange until the mid-19th century. The traders are now long gone, and the building is used as offices.

Above from far left: aerial view of Slotsholmen; the castle close-up.

Danish Parliament
The sessions of the Danish Parliament are open to the public. The Folketing can be found in the southern part of the main palace and is open Tue–Fri. In summer, there are free English tours at noon and 2pm. Enter through Parliament Yard.

Below: Neptune stands guard next to the Stock Exchange.

Above: Palace Church pews; Theatre Museum mannequin; the statue of Victoria, the goddess of victory, on top of the Thorvaldsen's Museum.

Royal Prisoner
Princess Leonora Christina was a favourite daughter of Christian IV. She spent almost 22 years in the Blue Tower after her husband Count Corfitz Ulfeldt plotted against the new king, Frederik III. Ulfeldt was accused of treason in 1663 but died before he could be executed.

Right: Thorvaldsen's Museum.

If you are visiting on a Sunday, between noon and 4pm, now would be a convenient time to make a short detour to visit the **Palace Church** ❸ (Christiansborg Slotskirke, Christiansborg Slotplads; www.ses.dk/ christiansborgpalace; free), the neoclassical building with the portico, on your right.

The present church, a lovely, light, airy affair, was built by C.F. Hansen between 1813 and 1826 after its Rococo predecessor burnt down in 1794. Almost 200 years later, in June 1992, during Whitsun Carnival, it was beset by fire again, its cupola and dome crashing to the floor. It has now been restored to international acclaim.

The Ruins of Absalon's Castle

Alternatively, visit the **ruins of Absalon's Castle** ❹ (tel: 33 92 64 92; May–Sept: daily 10am–5pm, Oct–Apr: Tue–Sun 10am–5pm; charge), which will give you an idea of the size as well as the history of this site. The entrance is on your right as you enter through the **Kings Gate** ❺, which was part of the fourth palace. As well as the remains of the walls, houses, a bakery and Absalon's chapel, you will be privy to Absalon's 'secret', an ancient toilet, through which detritus washed into the harbour. Look out, too, for a wooden pipe, which was part of a system of hollowed-out tree trunks that brought fresh water to the castle from Lake Emdrup 6km (4 miles) away. There are also some remains of the second castle, including the foundations of the terrible 'Blue Tower', in

which prisoners, noble and plebeian alike, could be holed up for years.

The State Rooms

The **State Rooms** ❻ (daily 10am–5pm, closed Mon Oct–Apr) are reached via the **Queen's Gate** ❼, which dates back to the time of the fourth palace. They are best visited on one of the recommended tours (in English 3pm), which include the **Throne Room**, the **Dining Room**, the **Royal Chambers**, the **Great Hall** with tapestries by Bjørn Nørgaard, and the **Queen's Reference Library** lined with roughly 3km (2 miles) of shelving. The guides are so enthusiastic that if you weren't before, you are bound to be a royalist by the time you finish the tour.

Thorvaldsen's Museum

If you are interested in classical 19th-century sculpture, from here, walk through Prince Jørgens Gård bearing

left to reach the **Thorvaldsen's Museum** ❽ (Bertel Thorvaldsens Plads 2; tel: 33 32 15 32; www.thorvaldsensmuseum.dk; Tue–Sun 10am–5pm; charge, Wed free) on the far edge of the island, on Gammel Strand *(see p.37)*. This brightly painted museum, its exterior depicting a life-size scene of the great sculptor's triumphant homecoming from Italy in 1838 after an absence of 40 years, houses virtually the entire collection of Bertel Thorvaldsen (1770–1844). His plans, casts, originals and replicas, plus his antiques – including examples of Egyptian, Greek, Etruscan and Roman works – and his collection of paintings, are all here. He is buried in the courtyard at the centre of the museum, which opened in 1848.

The Riding Ground

Back in the Inner Courtyard, look up at the tower that dominates the palace roofline; at 106m (348ft), it is one metre taller than the Town Hall and thus the highest in the old part of Copenhagen.

Now walk through to the **riding ground** ❾, which survived the fire of 1848. The equestrian statue, complementing the one in the palace forecourt, depicts **Christian IX** ❿ and is the work of sculptor, Anne Marie Carl Nielsen (1863–1945), wife of the Danish composer Carl Nielsen.

Theatre and Stable Museums

The Theatre and Stable Museums are under the arcade on the left-hand side of the riding ground. Both were part of the third palace and the sole survivors of the fire in 1794.

The **Theatre Museum** ⓫ (Christiansborg Ridebane 18; tel: 33 11 51 76; www.teatermuseet.dk; Tue–Thur 11am–3pm, Sat–Sun 1–4pm; charge, under-18s free) is not to be missed. One of the oldest court theatres in the world, it was designed by the French architect Nicolas-Henri Jardin and has been restored to how it would have looked in its sumptuous heyday between 1767 and 1881, when it was a stage for opera and drama. On a dramatic note, it is here that Christian VII's powerful adviser Struensee *(see box below)* was arrested for treason. Enhanced with mannequins and music, visitors can wander backstage, through the boxes,

The King's Doctor

Johann Struensee (1737–72) was a German doctor who was influenced by the revolutionary ideas of the Enlightenment. Convinced he had a greater calling than that of a mere physician, he sought preferment at court and, in 1767, became travelling doctor to the mentally unstable king, Christian VII. He gained the affection and trust of the young king and by September 1770, had been given the senior post of Privy Counsellor. By this time, he was also the lover of Queen Caroline Matilde (sister of George III, King of England), which caused great scandal. Until his downfall in January 1772, he ruled Denmark in the king's name, zealously, introducing over 1,000 reforms. But he was resented and his reforms met with disfavour. In January 1772, he was arrested, accused of usurping the royal authority in contravention of the royal law. He was imprisoned in Kastellet and executed on 28 April 1772.

Above: Stable Museum exhibit.

Palace Bridges

To reach Christiansborg Palace, you can cross one of nine bridges. The Rococo Marble Bridge (Marmorbroen), built in 1744, is the most ornate and was once part of Christian IV's Baroque palace. Originally the pavements were of Norwegian marble.

and stand on the stage, surrounded by props and other memorabilia.

The **Stable Museum** ⓬ (Christiansborg Ridebane 12; tel: 33 40 26 76; May–Sept: Fri–Sun 2–4pm, Oct–Apr: Sat–Sun 2–4pm; charge) next door houses the collection of state coaches and carriages in palatial, marble-columned surroundings that kept the king's horses in equine splendour. An astonishing 270 horses were housed here in 1789; now there are about 20 of them, and they can occasionally be seen in their stalls.

The Arsenal Museum

Turn left and walk towards the **Marble Bridge** ⓭. Cross over and have a bite at **Kanal Cafeen**, see ⓸⓵, or wait until you get to the Black Diamond.

For the **Arsenal Museum** ⓮ (Tøjhusmuseet; Tøjhusgade 3; Frederiksholmskanal; tel: 33 11 60 37; www.thm.dk; Tue–Sun noon–4pm; charge), cross the Marble Bridge, turn left and then right over **Prince's Bridge** (Prinsens Bro) into Tøjhusgade. Look to your right to see the outer walls of **Christian IV's Brewery** ⓯ (Bryghus), one of Copenhagen's oldest buildings.

The museum, about two-thirds of the way down on your right, is housed in a splendid brick building dating from 1598, which used to be Christian IV's cannon hall. It's worth a visit for the building alone – reputedly the longest in Europe at 163m (535ft) – not to mention the museum's staggering collection of weaponry ranging from inlaid duelling pistols to cannons. At the time of writing, a big renovation was underway: due for completion in 2013.

Old Royal Library and Danish Jewish Museum

Come out of the Arsenal and turn right down to **Parliament Yard** ⓰. Go through a door on your right where you will find an attractive **garden** ⓱, complete with pond and statuary (Søren Kirkegaard is on the right). At the far end is the **Old Royal Library** ⓲, dating from 1906.

The **Danish Jewish Museum** ⓳ (Holmens Kanal 2; tel: 33 11 22 18; www.jew mus.dk; Sept–May: Tue–Fri 1–4pm, Sat–Sun noon–5pm, June–Aug: Tue–Sun 10am–5pm; charge; children free) charts the life of the Jewish community in Copenhagen from the 17th century, when immigrants were rather

aristocratic, to just before World War II, when lower-class sections of society began to arrive to escape the hardships of Eastern Europe. The exhibition does not cover the Holocaust or World War II; this is covered at the Museum of Danish Resistance 1940–5 (Frihedsmuseet; *see p.51*).

The museum is also remarkable for its stunning interior, by the architect Daniel Libeskind. The design comprises interlocking sections, many of which tilt to one side, which are intended as a metaphor for the amicable history of the Jewish community and the Danes.

Black Diamond

The **Black Diamond** ➓ (Den Sorte Diamant; Christians Brygge 1; tel: 33 47 47 47; Mon–Fri 10am–5pm, Sat 10am–2pm; free) is the modern extension of the Royal Library and can be found on the opposite side of Christians Brygge, behind the old library building. Walk round via Tøjhusgade. It opened

in 1999 and takes its name from its shiny black exterior and slanting silhouette. It is best seen from a boat *(see p.46)*. See the press for details of exhibitions from the library's archives, which include original manuscripts by H.C. Andersen, Søren Kirkegaard and Karen Blixen. It is also home to the National Museum of Photography (with regular temporary exhibitions) and the Queen's Concert Hall. If you haven't had lunch yet, head to the minimalist, fat-free and very good **Søren K**, see ⑪②, on the ground floor.

Above from far left: canon line-up at the Arsenal Museum; Danish Jewish Museum; Stable Museum; the old library building.

Christian IV's Bryghus
Christian IV's brewery was originally built as part of Copenhagen's fortifications before it was turned into a brewery to supply beer to the navy.

$50 Million Book Theft

Some 4.5 million books are a lot to keep track of as Frede Møller-Kristensen, an employee of the Royal Library's Oriental department, realised. Between 1968 and 1978 he removed 3,200 items, including manuscripts by Martin Luther and first editions by Immanuel Kant, Thomas More and John Milton; nobody noticed until 1975. Møller-Kristensen sold over two million dollars' worth of books and remained undetected until his death in 2003. But his family were careless in selling the remainder and their cover was blown when books belonging to the library appeared at auction at Christie's in London. When the family house was raided in November 2003, 1,500 books were found. The family received sentences of between 18 months and three years each.

Food and Drink 🍴

① KANAL CAFEEN
Frederiksholms Kanal 18; tel: 33 11 57 70; Mon–Fri 11.30am–5pm, Sat 11.30am–3pm; € (cash only)
Hearty local food, including *smørrebrød* in warm and cosy wood-beamed surroundings.

② SØREN K
Søren Kirkegaard Plads 1; tel: 33 47 49 49; Mon–Sat noon–4pm, 5.30pm–10pm; €€€€
Come for the delicious food (French-Danish fusion) and the wonderful view through the large windows overlooking the harbour.

CHRISTIANSHAVN AND HOLMEN

Christianshavn is one of the city's most colourful areas and the closest you will get to seeing how Copenhagen looked before the fire in 1728. It was created as a harbourside merchant town to help promote trade.

Sea View
Harbour tours run from Nyhavn and from Gammel Strand (outside Slotskirke or Holmenskirke) and take you to Opera House and along Christianshavns Kanal, with Overgaden Oven Vandet (Upper Street Over the Water) and Overgaden Neden Vandet (Upper Street Below the Water) on either side, before returning to Slotsholmen (see p.76).

DISTANCE 3km (2 miles)
TIME A full day
START/END Knippel's Bridge
POINTS TO NOTE
If you find yourself short of time, an appealing way to see some of Christianshavn is to take a harbour tour *(see margin left).*

Christian IV wanted to make Copenhagen the cultural, religious and business centre for the whole of the Nordic region and, as such, needed to enhance the naval and trading capabilities of the city.

Between 1618 and 1623, he had fortifications built in the swampy area between Copenhagen and the island of Amager. Five bastions were completed by 1623. By 1639 he decided that he wanted to build a town and gave the order for Christianshavn (Christian's Harbour) to be built, allowing for dockyards and warehouses alongside the merchant housing. He was so determined for this new city to be populated that he offered many of Copenhagen's wealthy merchants independence, free land, 12 years unrestrained by taxes and several other

incentives to up sticks from their comfortable homes and business premises on the mainland and settle here instead.

His experiment worked and by the time he died in 1648, Copenhagen had become the naval and economic centre of the region.

CHRISTIAN'S CHURCH

Start at the green-towered **Knippel's Bridge ❶** (Knippelsbro), the site of the first bridge between the mainland and Amager Island. Built in 1937, it is named after Hans Knipp, the tollkeeper of the first bridge erected in 1618. Note the six black, shiny buildings on your right, designed by the architect Henning Larsen, in stark contrast with the old-world atmosphere of the rest of the area. Walk up as far as Strandgade and take a right and walk down to Christian's Church.

Christian's Church ❷ (Christians Kirke; Strandgade 1; tel: 32 54 15 76; Tue–Fri 10am–4pm; free) is one of two splendid churches on Christianshavn. It was built in 1754–9 by Nicolai Eigtved, Frederik V's master architect, who designed many of Copenhagen's 18th-century churches. This elegant rococo church is notable for its unusual, the-

atrical layout in which three tiers of seating galleries run around the walls, with the royal pew in the centre opposite the altar, technically in the position of the 'stage'. Originally named Frederiks Kirke, the church's name was changed in 1901 to reflect the importance of Christian IV. Today, it's also known as the Theatre Church, and is sometimes used as a concert venue, for example, during the Jazz Festival.

STRANDGADE AND THE DOCKS

Walk back up to Torvegade and cross over into **Strandgade ❸**. This elegant 17th-century street was the one of the earliest, and **Nos 30** and **32** were the first houses to be built here. They originally had curved attic gables similar to those adorning Rosenborg Castle; these have since been replaced by an additional storey. The painter Vilhelm Hammershøi *(see p.97)* lived at No. 30 between 1899 and 1909, producing many of his trademark grey-tone interiors here.

As its name, Beach Street, suggests, Strandgade was originally right on the shoreline, with jetties and harbourside gardens. The closer to the water (and Copenhagen) you were, the smarter the address. It still has a certain cachet today: the 'world's best restaurant', Noma, lies at its furthest end.

Go through a wooden door on the left, opposite Sankt Annæ Gade, into **Asiatisk Plads ❹**. This is named for

Above from far left: capturing serene Christianshavn.

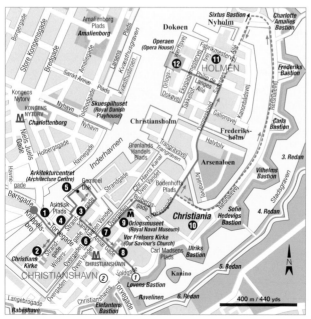

Below: Christian's Church adornments.

Above: Our Saviour's Church altarpiece; tranquil Christianshavn.

The Order of the Elephant

This is an ancient order and the highest in Denmark. It was instituted in its current form in 1693 by Christian V. Royalty and heads of state may belong; the billionaire industrialist Mærsk Mc-Kinney Møller is the only living commoner to be a member. Nicolas Ceaucescu, late former Romanian dictator, is the only head of state to have had the honour revoked.

the Asiatisk Kompagnie, which traded with India and China from here in the 18th century. It was also responsible for commissioning and paying for the excessively expensive statue in the Amalienborg Plads *(see p.49)*. On the north side, the marble façade of the elongated rococo warehouse was designed by Nicolai Eigtved in 1750 and dates from Christianshavn's heyday. It is now a conference centre.

Walk past the lovely old boats and bear right, past the end of the next building into **Gammel Dok** (Old Dock). On the far side is the **Architecture Centre ❺** (Arkitekturcentret; Strandgade 27B; tel: 32 57 19 30; www.dac.dk; daily 10am–5pm, late opening Wed until 9pm; charge), Denmark's foremost exhibition centre for new architecture. Housed in a lovely old converted warehouse with exposed beams, it has constantly changing exhibitions. It also has a good bookshop and its café has an excellent waterside view. Further up on **Grønlands Handels Plads** opposite Nyhavn, the warehouses belonged to the Royal Greenland Trading Company (Kongelig Grøn-

landske Handel) and were used to store whale oil, skins and dried fish. There was then, and still is now, a Greenlandic population in Christianshavn.

Walk back down Strandgade to Sankt Annæ Gade; note **No. 32** on the corner of the junction, thought to be the oldest house in Christianshavn, dating from *c*.1622. Follow Sankt Annæ Gade to the two lovely cobbled streets overlooking the houseboats on the **Christianshavn Canal: Overgaden Neden Vandet ❻** (Upper Street Below the Water) is on your left and **Overgaden Oven Vandet ❼** (Upper Street Above the Water) on your right. Cross the bridge and head towards **Our Saviour's Church**, with the twisting, golden spire.

OUR SAVIOUR'S CHURCH

Our Saviour's Church ❽ (Vor Frelsers Kirke; Sankt Annæ Garde 29; tel: 32 54 68 83; www.vorfrelserskirke.dk; spire July–Aug: daily 10am–7pm; June: daily 10am–4pm; Apr–May & Sept–mid-Dec: daily 11am–4pm; charge) is the oldest church in Christianshavn, built by Christian V for the inhabitants of the new harbour district between 1682 and 1694. Dedicated to Our Saviour, it is a wonderful example of Dutch Baroque style and is particularly well known for its spiralling tower, which twists to a height of 90m (295ft). The view from the top of the external stairway is exhilarating but the climb is not for the unfit or acrophobic – the pine-wood structure almost seems to sway in strong winds. Above you is a golden ball and a 3m (10ft) figure of

> ### Food and Drink 🍴
> **① BASTIONEN AND LØVEN**
>
> Lille Mølle Christianshavn, Voldgade 50; tel: 32 95 09 40; www.bastionen-loven.dk; Mon–Sat 11am–10pm, Sun 10am–4.30pm; €–€€€
> This charming restaurant is in an old mill on the ramparts of Christianshavn. It serves excellent Danish food and is especially popular for its weekend brunches (10am–2pm).

Christ (reputedly the ugliest statue in Copenhagen!).

Inside is a light-filled, white-walled church with tall windows in the shape of a Greek cross. The cherub-covered font has a sad history: it was given by Frederik IV's childless, morganatic wife in 1702; she died in childbirth in 1704, and her baby died nine months later. The altarpiece, inspired by the altar in the Roman church of S.S. Domenico e Sisto, shows God (represented by the sun) and the events of Maundy Thursday, when Christ prayed that he should be spared the crucifixion. Christian V's insignia can be seen on the entrance, the ceiling and the three-storey organ, which rests on two elephants, the emblem of Denmark's most prestigious order *(see margin left)*, founded in 1450. The pulpit dates from 1773 and is decorated with figures of the apostles.

Turn left out of the church and walk to the end of the road; bear left up onto the fortifications, and on your right is one of Christianshavn's best restaurants, **Bastionen and Løven**, see ⑪①.

ROYAL NAVAL MUSEUM

Retrace your steps and walk down Overgaden Oven Vandet, passing the **Royal Naval Museum** ❾ (Orlogsmuseet; Overgaden Oven Vandet 58–64; tel: 33 11 60 37; www.orlogsmuseet.dk; Tue–Sun noon–4pm; charge except Wed) on your right. Although there's little information in English here, there are some beautiful 17th-century model ships, as well as uniforms, nautical instruments and weapons. The long, rococo-style building was formerly used as a school, a prison, a hospital and then a rehabilitation centre for wounded naval personnel.

CHRISTIANIA

If you wish to visit **Christiania** ❿, take Brobergsgade, the second right

Above from far left: the view from Our Saviour's Church; walking through Christiania; the spiralling tower of Our Saviour's Church; Christiania mural.

Left: young skater showing off his skills.

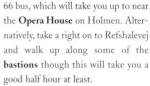

Night at the Opera
To go to the opera house directly from the centre, take harbour buses Nos. 992 or 993 from Nyhavn, or the metro to Christianshavns Torv and the No. 66 bus; a water bus also runs after each performance, but queues can be long, and the No. 66 might be a better bet if you find yourself at the back of the queue.

after the Royal Naval Museum, and then keep walking until you end up on Prinsessegade. Opposite is the colourful mural-covered entrance to Copenhagen's 'Free State', a 19th-century, ex-army barracks that was taken over by freethinkers in 1971.

Christiania is home to just over 1,000 people, out a population in Christianshavn of 9,000. To get the most out of it, take a tour (www.rundvisergruppen.dk; July–Aug: daily 3pm, Sept–June: Sat–Sun 3pm); just wandering around can be a little underwhelming.

HOLMEN

From here retrace your steps and take a right up Prinsessegade. The quickest thing to do here is to wait for a No.

66 bus, which will take you up to near the **Opera House** on Holmen. Alternatively, take a right on to Refshalevej and walk up along some of the **bastions** though this will take you a good half hour at least.

Holmen ⑪ is made up of five man-made islands (now connected by bridges), which were created from 1690 for the royal navy. It is built on muddy landfill that was dredged up by convicts who walked in huge treadmills in the waterway between Copenhagen and Amager. Eventually, the authorities supplied a horse-drawn dredger. Parts of the islands rest on ships that have been sunk and filled with boulders.

Nyholm, the first island, was built to replace the naval dock at Gammel-holm, which had become too small and the water too shallow for the navy's fleet of ever-larger and faster ships. The **Sixtus Bastion** at its far end is still the place from which cannon are fired in salute, and there are several unique historical buildings still standing.

Once Holmen was a working naval base, its workers came across the water every day from Nyboder *(see p.53)*. They were considered so important that during the plague in 1711–12, which killed a third of the population, they lived in huts on Nyholm to keep them away from infection.

The navy remained on Holmen for three centuries until it finally, and regret-fully, closed its base in 1993. Since then, the area has seen an increase in public spaces and housing and is now also home to four art schools and a brand new, impressive opera house.

Opera House

Opposite the Amalienborg is Copenhagen's exciting new **Opera House** ⑫ (Operaen; Ekvipagemestervej 10; tel: 33 69 69 69; www.operaen.dk; charge for guided tours only). Opinions regarding its strikingly contemporary design (by Henning Larsen) vary, especially with regard to its controversial position on the 'Golden Axis' with the Amalienborg and the Marble Church on the other side of the harbour. But whatever the critics say, the building is impressive, standing 14 storeys high (five underground), with a flat grey roof that blends in with the sky.

Inside, a large glass-fronted foyer looks out over the water, lit by several huge, one-tonne lamps by Danish-Icelandic artist Olafur Eliasson, who constructed them from thousands of pieces of glass that change colour depending on the temperature. In the centre, the main auditorium is encased in Canadian walnut and looks like a huge wooden pumpkin. Inside, it is a masterpiece of acoustic design, with an elaborate gold-leaf ceiling made of over 100,000 pieces of 23.75-carat gold.

The building took four years to build and was a gift to the nation by the A.P. Møller Foundation, established in 1953 by a wealthy Danish shipping magnate. The behind-the-scenes tour is very interesting; the areas you see depend on rehearsal schedules, but there are over 1,100 rooms in the building, so you won't be stuck for something to see. If you are lucky you will get to stand on the stage itself.

From here, hop on a harbour bus and go back to Knippel's Bridge. If you enjoy being afloat, you could now see Christianshavn's canals from the water by hiring a rowing boat (as Copenhageners have done since the 19th century) from Christianshavns Bådudlejning & Cafe (Overgaden Neden Vandet; tel: 29 32 96 53 53; June–Aug: 9am–midnight); or while away your time in the local shops and cafés, notably **L'Altro**, see ⑪②.

Above from far left: the maritime way of life at Christianshavn is still there for all to see; the striking new Opera House opened in 2005.

Holmen 5
The five islands that make up Holmen are Nyholm, Dokøen, Frederiksholm, Arsenaløen and Christiansholm.

Below left and right: the stylish interior of the Opera House is a showcase of modern Danish design.

Food and Drink

② L'ALTRO
Torvegade 62; tel: 32 54 54 06; www.laltro.dk; Mon–Sat 6pm–midnight (kitchen closes at 10pm); €€
Owned by the same brothers who own nearby Michelin-starred Era Ora, this offers excellent, traditional, home-made Italian food.

ROSKILDE

Seaside Roskilde is a relaxing day out just 25 minutes away by train. It is considerably older than Copenhagen and for centuries was much more important. This walk takes you to the town's highlights, the cathedral and Viking Ship Museum, via ancient sights and then back through the park.

DISTANCE 5km (3 miles)
TIME A full day
START Railway Station
END Church of Our Lady
POINTS TO NOTE
If you are short of time, concentrate on the cathedral and the Viking Museum. Also note that restaurants serve lunch until about 3pm and don't serve again until about 5pm.

Roskilde is thought to have been founded in the 10th century by the splendidly named Harold Bluetooth (Harold I) of Denmark, a Viking who converted to Christianity *c*.AD 960. It is well placed at the bottom of a fjord, and tucked away but with access to the North Sea. Harold established his court here and also built a church on the site of the current cathedral.

By 1020, Roskilde was a bishopric, and in 1158, Bishop Absalon, who later founded Copenhagen, became bishop of Roskilde. He established several more churches and monasteries, until there were 14 parish churches and five convents and monasteries in addition to a brick church on the site of the present cathedral. In the Middle Ages, Roskilde was one of the largest, most important cities in Northern Europe, with between 5,000 and 10,000 inhabitants and thousands of visiting pilgrims each year.

TO THE CATHEDRAL

From the Italian-inspired station, which dates from 1847, turn right up Jerbanegade. The wall on your left encloses **Gråbrødre Kirkegård ❶**, an attractive church surrounded by a graveyard now used as a park, which stands on the site of a 13th-century complex belonging to the Franciscans. Take a look at the beautiful view through the gates or turn left down Store Gråbrødretorvstræde if you want to enter the park.

Walk across cobbled Hestetorvet ❷ named for the horse market that was held here in the 12th century, just inside the ramparts by the eastern gate, where you cannot miss the **Roskilde Jars**. These are the work of artist Peter Brandes and stand 5m (16ft) high and weigh 24 tonnes. They were gifted to the city in 1998 on its 1,000th anniversary by a local firm, and, as they are both storage jars and urns, represent Life and Death.

Pass between the café and the pharmacy to the shopping street, **Algade ❸**,

Above from far left:
St James' church;
Roskilde Palace; royal
throne; Roskilde in its
winter coat.

an ancient street that has been paved for over 700 years. Before you follow the route down Sankt Peders Stræde, wander along Algade to look at medieval paving just beyond the Hotel Prindsen; the imposing red-brick 17th-century apothecary's building; and the old merchant's house opposite at No. 9. There is a good family restaurant **Bryggergården**, see ①①, at No. 15; go through its archway to see the timbered backs of the old houses. Also, have a look through the gates of No. 31 to see the back of the Old Priory, which you will see shortly at closer quarters. Now turn down Sankt Peders Stræde until you reach **Roskilde Priory** on your right.

Roskilde Priory

Roskilde Priory ❹ (Roskildekloster; Sankt Peders Stræde 8; tel: 46 35 02 19; www.roskildekloster.dk; by tour only, ring for details; charge), was built in 1565 in Dutch Renaissance style as a manor house. It stands on the site of a former medieval priory, which was destroyed during the Reformation in 1536 – its bricks were sold off and reused in many of Roskilde's buildings. Shortly after it was built, the manor house was bought by the widows of

two Danish war heroes and run as a home for unmarried noblewomen: they lived in great style, as a tour of the Great Hall, abbey church and reception rooms will show.

Roskilde Museum

Out of the Priory, cross the road and walk down Sankt Ols Stræde; you can see the spires of the cathedral ahead of you. Keep walking straight on if you want to visit the tourist office; otherwise turn right at the end and the **Roskilde Museum ❺** (Sankt Ols Gade 18; tel: 46 31 65 29; www.roskilde museum.dk; daily 11am–4pm; charge). The museum offers over 6,000 arte-

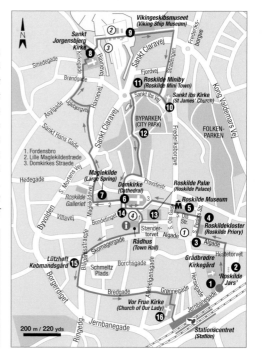

Food and Drink 🍴

① RESTAURANT BRYGGERGÅRDEN

Algade 15; tel: 46 35 01 03;
www.restaurantbryggergaarden.dk;
daily 11am–11pm; €
Good solid food served up in a cosy
pub-like restaurant with helpful staff.

facts relating to the history of Roskilde and nearby Lejre, from prehistoric times until the 1970s, including the founding of the annual Roskilde rock festival *(see margin left)*.

THE CATHEDRAL

From here, cross over Sankt Ols Gade into Domkirkes Stræde. Turn left and pass in front of the cathedral for the main entrance; visit now or on your way back from the Viking Ship Museum.

The **cathedral** (Domkirke; Apr–Sept: Mon–Sat 9am–4.45pm, Sun 12.30pm–4.45pm, Oct–Mar: Tue–Sat 10am–3.45pm, Sun 12.30pm–3.45pm; closed during services; charge) is a Unesco World Heritage Site and one of the earliest brick-built buildings in Northern Europe. Pick up an information sheet on your way in so you have a plan of the building.

Work on the church began in the 1170s, under Bishop Absalon, but the building was completed by his successor Peder Sunesøn, who was aware of the new Gothic style that was then emerging in France. (Indeed, this is one of the earliest Gothic buildings outside France.) The cathedral is famous for being the resting place of the 39 Danish kings and queens, going back to the Middle Ages; their chapels and tombs are a fascinating display of changes in style. There are also **pillar tombs** in the sanctuary behind the choir, of royals (including Harald Bluetooth) who were originally buried in the two, possibly three, earlier churches that have stood on this site.

Inside, you are greeted with a white, airy interior with bare brick columns, medieval frescoes and some Renaissance furniture, including the pulpit, organ and altar. Before the Reformation in 1536, the nave would have been empty of pews or pulpit; instead there were 75 side chapels where mass was said daily for the souls of the dead. On your left, on the wall to the left of the west window, don't miss the **mechanical clock** with figures of St George and the Dragon that re-enact the dragon's defeat and death cries on the hour.

The frescoes in the **Chapel of the Magi** on the south side are some of the best and date from 1462. This is also where you'll find the unique 'King's Pillar', where visiting kings stood to be measured – Peter the Great's height marker is the highest by far. Opposite, on the north side, are two medieval chapels that were given startling new decorations in 2010. St Andrew's Chapel gained a glittering new altarpiece by artist Peter Brandes, while in St Birgitte's Chapel, you'll find a very modern sarcophagus, designed by Bjørn Nørgaard, which will eventually hold the present queen Margrethe and her husband.

The oldest frescoes are found at the east (altar) end and were part of the pre-Reformation, Catholic side chapels. On the north side of the **ambulatory**, note the fresco depicting Bishop Absalon and a little further to the south, the tomb of the three-legged 'ghost horse', said to be jet black with blazing red eyes, the sight of which was an omen of one's impending demise.

Roskilde Rocks
Inspired by Woodstock in 1969, Roskilde has held an annual festival since 1971 (www.roskildefestival.dk). It ranks alongside Glastonbury in the rock calendar and has featured international and local artists such as Blur, Björk, the Scissor Sisters, Fat Boy Slim and rock legends Bob Dylan and Nirvana.

Good v. Evil
Carved angels like this one fill the Gothic cathedral – but can you find the small green devil who, armed with pen and ink, is writing down the names of anyone who is misbehaving?

The **choir** has an ornate Renaissance altar piece that features scenes from the New Testament. Also here is the tomb of Denmark's first queen regnant, Margrethe I – the little bells hanging from her clothing were all the rage in the 15th century. There are also some beautiful stalls here, carved with scenes from the Old Testament on the south side and New Testament on the north, with odd little trolls wandering through the narrative.

TO THE VIKING MUSEUM

Coming out of the cathedral, turn right, looking towards the sea. Cross Skolegade and head into leafy Lille Maglekildestræde. This takes you past the **Maglekilde** ❼ (Large Spring), on your right, inside a wooden well house that dates from 1927 and topped by an older mermaid weathervane. In the 19th century, this spring supplied water for five mills in industrialised Roskilde; it now yields one sixth of what it used to.

At the end of the road, turn right onto Maglekildevej, where you'll see the spring's water gushing out of the mouth of a head of Neptune. Walk past the **Roskilde Galleriet**, a commercial art gallery, until you reach Sankt Claravej, lined with 17th-century cottages. Turn right and first left on to Havnevej and then left again onto Uglebjergvej.

St Jorgensberg's Church

At the junction, turn right onto Asylgade, which then turns into the pretty Kirkegade, with **St Jorgensbjerg**

Church ❽ (Sankt Jorgensbjerg Kirke; July–mid-Aug: Mon–Fri 10am–noon; www.sjk.dk; free) on your right.

This is Denmark's oldest intact stone building, with a choir and nave dating from the 11th century. Pop in if it is open; inside, there is a 19th-century votive ship model, a 16th-century crucifix and the remains of a 'leper's space' in the north wall, where people with leprosy received communion through a knee-high hole in the wall.

Walk through the churchyard, looking out over the lovely view of the fjord, and then down the steps until you come out on Havnevej. Turn right, then immediately left onto the harbourside, where you'll then see the wooden buildings of the **Viking Ship Museum** in front of you.

VIKING SHIP MUSEUM

Arguably the highlight of a trip to Roskilde is the excellent **Viking Ship Museum** ❾ (Vikingeskibsmuseet;

Above from far left: the cathedral's Gothic chapel and royal tombs, which mark out Danish history through the graves of generations of monarchs; reflecting outside the cathedral.

Shorter Route If you want to save time, follow the signs from Skolegade for a more direct route to the Viking Ship Museum.

Below: picturesque Lille Maglekildestræde.

Harbour Picnic
Roskilde's peaceful harbour is filled with white sails. There are several benches, and it's a nice place for a picnic, although there are also picnic tables in the museum if you prefer.

Roskilde Harbour; tel: 46 30 02 00; www.vikingeskibsmuseet.dk; July–Aug: daily 10am–5pm; Sept–June daily 10am–4pm; charge), passionately dedicated to Viking ships and sailing. The core exhibits are five well-preserved boats that were discovered in 1962 in the channel close to Skuldelev, 20km (12 miles) north of Roskilde. They had been deliberately scuttled – over a thousand years ago – to create an underwater blockade against raiders.

As well as seeing the originals in the beautifully designed Viking Ship Hall, you can step aboard re-creations of the boats at the jetty, constructed in the museum's boatyard using traditional Viking methods and materials. You can also experience a Viking raider or trader's life for yourself by rowing out into the fjord in one of the evocative, creaking wooden ships (May–Sept: sailing times vary; tel: 46 30 02 53 for details and bookings).

For lunch, there are two options, a restaurant boat, **MS Sagafjord**, see ⓩ②, or the museum restaurant, **Snekken**, see ⓩ③, near the entrance.

BACK TO TOWN

To take a different route back, turn left out of the museum. When you get to Strandengen, turn right and follow the road to the junction with Sankt Ibs Vej. **St James' Church** ❿ (Skt Ibs Kirke), a ruin with roots in the 12th century, stands on your left. Turn right and follow the road round until you come to **Roskilde Mini Town** ⓫ on your right, another millennium gift to the town in 1998. The model shows Roskilde as it was in the 14th century.

Cross the road and enter the **City Park** ⓬ (Byparken), the site of various medieval archaeological remains, through a gate on your left. Walk up through the park for about 500m, heading for the cathedral. It is easy to see its variety of architectural styles from this side. Don't forget to look back at the sea, with the ships' masts pointing skyward in the distance.

Walk round the cathedral into Domkirke Pladsen. If you haven't yet eaten, there is a nice little cellar restaurant, **Radhus Kaelderen**, see ⓩ④, on the corner of Fordensbro.

Walk down Fordensbro into Stændertorvet, the main square, which was laid out as it is now in 1908. On your left stands the golden-walled **Roskilde Palace** ⓭ (Stændertorvet 3), a rather modest Baroque palace dating from the 1730s and built on the site of a medieval

---

Vikings Return to Dublin

The largest of the five Viking ships found in the fjord and now showcased in the Viking Museum is *Skuldelev 2*, a 30m (100ft), ocean-going warship that was originally built in Dublin *c*.1040. She was reconstructed between 2000 and 2004 and, named

Havhingsten fra Glendalough (The Sea Stallion from Glendalough), set sail back to Dublin on 1 July 2007 with a crew of 70. She arrived, seven weeks and 1,852km (1,000 nautical miles) later, on 16 August.

bishop's palace. Sections of the building are accessible to visitors: including the excellent **Museum of Contemporary Art** (Museet for Samtidskunst; tel: 46 31 65 70; Tue–Fri 11am–5pm; Sat–Sun noon–4pm; charge, free Wed), with two floors of changing exhibitions. It focuses on art from the 1950s onwards, with a particular interest in sound and video installations. The **Palace Wing** (tel: 46 32 14 70; Tue–Sun noon–4pm), opens for occasional art exhibitions; you can probably skip the small local-history museum based in a third wing.

On the right is the **Town Hall** ⓮, dating from 1884. Note its splendid tower (c.1550), the only remaining part of the 12th-century church of St Laurentius. You can visit the ruins of the church, preserved under the square – ask the tourist office, inside the town hall, for the key.

BACK TO THE STATION

To return to the station, turn right out of the square down the shopping street Skomagergade. Continue to the end and take a left down Ringstedgade. On the right is **Lützhøft Købmandsgård** ⓯ (Ringstedgade 6–8; Mon–Fri 11am–5pm, Sat 10am–2pm), an old merchant's house with a charming shop that is reminiscent of the 1920s, and the Museum of Tools, with a collection from the period 1840–1950.

Keep on until you reach Bredgade. Turn left and carry on, crossing Allehelgensgade on to Grønnegarde. Turn right into Fruegade. The **Church of Our Lady** stands on your right.

Dating from the late 11th century, the **Church of Our Lady** ⓰ (Vor Frue Kirke; tel: 46 35 58 14) was an important, wealthy church – so much so that St Margaret of Højelse, a relative of Bishop Absalon, was buried here in 1177. It was also connected to a Cistercian convent that was built close by in 1160. The convent was abolished in 1536, and its buildings and the eastern end of the church were demolished around forty years later. It has a pretty white-washed interior and the 17th-century pews were carved by Casper Luebbeke, Master of Roskilde.

Turn right out of the church and at the end, turn left onto Jernbanegade. The station is a little further along on your right.

Food and Drink 🍴

② MS SAGAFJORD
Roskilde Harbour; tel: 46 75 64 60; www.sagafjord.dk; Apr–Oct: Thur–Sun 1–3pm, 6–9.30pm, May–Sept: daily 1–3pm, 6–9.30pm; €
Buffet or menu cruising in Viking waters along the Roskilde Fjord.

③ RESTAURANT SNEKKEN
Vindeboder 16; tel: 46 35 98 16; www.snekken.dk; 11.30am–10pm; €–€€
Café or restaurant meals in lovely, airy venue with views over the water.

④ RADHUS KAELDEREN
Fondensbro 1; tel: 46 36 01 00; www.raadhuskaelderen.dk; Mon–Sat 11am–11pm; €€
Good restaurant in the cellar of the town hall, with traditional Danish food. Seating in the small courtyard in summer.

Above from far left: reconstructions of Viking ships are used to take visitors for a trip on the fjord in the summer; Viking coins.

Family Excursion Kids can paddle canoes, build fires and explore an Iron-Age village at Sagnlandet Lejre (tel: 46 48 08 78; www.sagnlandet.dk; see website for opening hours; charge), a fabulous archaeology centre 13km (8 miles) from Roskilde.

Below: day trippers ready to explore Roskilde; one of five perfectly restored Viking ships.

HELSINGØR

Famous for its fictional association with William Shakespeare's Hamlet, Helsingør (Elsinore) is a charming town on the banks of the Sound, just 6.5km (4 miles) away from Sweden aross the water.

Visitor Info
The tourist office (Havnepladsen 3; tel: 49 21 13 33; www.visitnordsjaelland .com; Mon–Fri 10am–4pm, Sat 10am–2pm in July) is handily located near' the railway station. If you have a Copenhagen Card, it will get you into the town museum, the Technical Museum and the museums in Kronborg Castle.

DISTANCE 3km (1¾ miles); further if visiting Technical Museum
TIME A half/full day
START Railway Station
END Technical Museum
POINTS TO NOTE
You will need to do some careful planning to squeeze everything on this tour in. You may find it more convenient to do the tour in the opposite order.

Helsingør is an historic town, with entire streets of well-preserved, colour-washed buildings. From the station, cross Havnepladsen, and turn right along Strandgade (Beach Street) to

Skibsklarerergården ❶ (Strandgade 91; tel: 49 28 18 36; www.museerne. helsingor.dk; admission by tour only: Tue–Fri noon, 1pm, 2pm & 3pm, Sat 10am, 11am, noon & 1pm; charge), a former grocers and ship chandlers, originally dating from the 16th century. If you are ready for lunch, go back along Strandgade to Bramstræde and turn right to Stengade, the main pedestrian street, which is full of restaurants; check out **Madam Sprunck**, see ⑪①.

KRONBORG CASTLE

Walk down to Havnegade. Turn left and walk round the dock in the direction of the castle towers. On the way, you'll pass the Culture Yard (Kulturværftet), containing a library, playhouse and good restaurant, which was built to regenerate Helsingør's disused shipyards. **Kronborg Castle ❷** (Kronborg Slot; tel: 49 21 30 78; www.kronborgslot.dk; May–Sept: daily 10.30am–5pm, Apr & Oct: Tue–Sun 11am–4pm, Nov–Mar: Tue–Sun 11am–3pm; charge) is a magnificent Renaissance-style edifice, originally built in 1420 as a fortress to protect the town and to encourage trading ships to pay King Erik V the 'Sound Dues' that he demanded for sailing in these waters. It is famous as the model for Shakespeare's 'Elsinore' in

Hamlet. It has a massive banqueting hall and some suitably miserable dungeons.

SANKT ANNA GADE

Head back onto Havnegade, taking a right up Kongensgade and then first left in Sankt Anna Gade, an ancient street of much historical interest.

Carmelite Priory and City Museum

On your left is the **Carmelite Priory ❸** (Karmeliterklosteret; Sankt Anna Gade 38; tel: 49 21 17 74; www.sctmariae.dk; mid-May–mid-Sept: Tue–Sun 10am–3pm, mid-Sept–mid-May: daily 10am–2pm), a fine building dating from the mid-15th century. Its church (St Maria's/ Sankt Maria Kirke) is decorated with recently restored frescoes dating from 1480–90, and the splendid Baroque organ dates from 1662–3.

Next door, in another priory building erected in 1516 as a sailors' hospital, the **City Museum ❹** (Bymuseum; Sankt Anna Gade 36; tel: 49 28 18 00; www.museerne.helsingor.dk; Tue–Fri & Sun noon–4pm, Sat 10am–2pm; charge) has an interesting history, a Renaissance banqueting hall on the first floor and a mix of exhibits.

The Cathedral

Continue down the street and one block on on the same side you will see Helsingør's recently renovated red-brick Gothic **cathedral ❺** (Helsingør Domkirke; Sankt Anna Gade 12; tel: 49 21 04 43; www.helsingordomkirke.dk; May–Aug: 10am–4pm, Sept–Apr: 10am–2pm).

Originally a small Romanesque church dating from *c*.1200, this was the first church in Helsingør. The current building dates from 1559 and was made a cathedral in 1961. It contains a particularly fine 15th-century crucifix, a Renaissance pulpit (1568) and an exuberantly carved wooden altarpiece, decorated with gold leaf.

Technical Museum

It's worth heading to the far end of town for the **Technical Museum ❻** (Danmarks Tekniske Museum; Fabriksvej 25; tel: 49 22 26 11; www.tekniskmuseum.dk; Tue–Sun 10am–5pm; Mon late June–mid Aug; charge), which is full of captivating vehicles, gadgets and appliances, including more than 30 aeroplanes, some of which belonged to Jacob Ellehammer (1871–1946), who designed and flew his own aeroplane in 1906, making him one of the first European pilots.

To reach the museum from Helsingør station, catch bus No. 805 in the direction of Espergærde and ask the bus driver to stop at Fabriksvej; the stop is right outside the museum.

Above from far left: spectacular Kronborg Castle inspired Shakespeare no less; typical colour-washed houses; castle detail.

Experimentarium
If you have time, visit the Experimentarium (Tuborg Havnevej 7, DK-2900 Hellerup; tel: 39 27 33 33; www.experimentarium.dk; Mon, Wed–Fri 9.30am–5pm, Tue 9.30am–9pm, Sat–Sun 11am–5pm; charge, 0–2s free), an interactive science centre that is great fun for kids. Get off the S train to/from Helsingør at Hellerup Station: take bus 166, which stops directly outside the Experimentarium.

ART TOUR

There are three world-class art galleries outside Copenhagen that it would be a pity to miss. With time, planning and a willingness to walk, you can combine two of them in one trip.

DISTANCE n/a

TIME A full day

START Ørdrupsgaard

END Louisiana

POINTS TO NOTE

These are not the easiest places to combine as public transport isn't direct but if you time it properly, you should make reasonable time. Try to do the trip Tue–Fri if you can, as Louisiana stays open then until 11pm. If you want to check timetables and routes, visit http://www.rejseplanen.dk.

Other Options

Two big family attractions in Klampenborg are the white-sand Bellevue Beach, two minutes' walk from the station; and Dyrehaven, a lovely forested deer park which is home to the world's oldest funfair, Bakken (www.bakken.dk; end Mar–Sept). Denmark's Aquarium (Akvarium; Kavaler-gården 1; tel: 39 62 32 83; www.akvarium.dk; June–Aug: 10am–6pm; Feb–May & Sept–Oct: 10am–5pm; Nov–Jan: 10am–4pm; charge) is based near Ørdrupsgaard until 2013 (after which it moves to Amager, near the airport); take bus No. 388.

ØRDRUPGAARD

Just 8km (5 miles) out of Copenhagen, this is perhaps the only trip when a car would be handy. Otherwise, put your walking boots on. The best way to **Ørdrupsgaard ❶** (Vilvordevej 110,

Charlottenlund; tel: 39 64 11 83; www.ordrupgaard.dk; Tue and Thur–Fri 1–5pm; Wed 1–7pm; Sat–Sun 11am–5pm; charge) is to take either the S-Tog or the regional Kystbanen line to Klampenborg Station (20 mins), then take bus No. 388 to Vilvordevej (5 mins). If you prefer to walk the 1.5km from the station, go down the stairs from the platform and turn left out of the station (not on the beach side). Follow the road for about 250m (273 yards), turn left onto Christian-sholmsvej, then right onto Klampenborgvej. After about 1.3km (1 mile), turn left onto Vilvordevej. (An alternative train journey is to take

Food and Drink

① LOUISIANA CAFE

Gammel Strandvej 13; Tue–Fri 11am–9.30pm, Sat–Sun 11am–5.30pm; €–€€

Sit by the fire in winter or by the water in summer in this very pleasant café. Snacks and sandwiches are served all day, with a hot-and-cold buffet at lunch and in the evening.

the S-Tog to Lyngby, then the same bus – No. 388 – to Vilvordevej.)

Ørdrupgaard is a lovely old house with a striking modern extension, full of Danish and European Impressionist paintings, with lots of premier-league artists, including Cézanne, Degas, Manet and Monet. There is also a delightful collection of paintings by Danish artist Vilhelm Hammershøi. Allow yourself plenty of time to tour the collection, as the free audio guide is thorough, and there is a pretty garden and a pleasant **café**. Design fans should also take a look at the house of visionary Danish furniture designer and architect Finn Juhl (1912–89), which borders Ørdrupgaard park and became part of the art museum in 2008.

LOUISIANA

Walk (or take the No. 388 bus) to Klampenborg station. From here, take an S-Tog to Humlebæk (direction Helsingør); these run regularly. The journey takes about 25 minutes, and then it's a 20-minute, signposted walk.

The wonderful **Louisiana Modern Art Museum ❷** (Gammel Strandvej 13, Humlebæk; tel: 49 19 07 19; www.louisiana.dk; Tue–Fri 11am–10pm, Sat–Sun 11am–6pm; charge) is a work of art in itself. Several parts are buried into the hilly slopes, so you'll descend underground only to pop out unexpectedly into the sunlit sculpture garden. Numerous glass walls also blur the boundaries between art and nature, and much of the time you will find yourself as aware of the beautiful land-

scape and sea views outside as you are of the art inside.

The impressive permanent collection features work by artists including Arp, Francis Bacon, Calder, Dubuffet, Max Ernst, Sam Francis, Giacometti, Kiefer, Henry Moore, Picasso, and Warhol. Giacometti's marvellous collection of 13 elongated figures is a highlight. The excellent **café,** see ⑪①, overlooking the Sound (sit outside in summer) is another incentive for making the trip and is a good place to have supper.

Arke

On the Baltic Coast is the **Arken Modern Art Museum ❸** (Arken Museet for Moderne Kunst; Skovej 100, Ishøj; tel: 43 54 02 22; for special tours tel: 43 57 34 55; Tue & Thur–Sun 10am–5pm, Wed 10am–9pm; charge), a marvellous building in the shape of a ship's hull that provides an ideal setting for the avant-garde works of art displayed here. An extension has recently been added, allowing the museum to hang a permanent exhibition – which includes a room dedicated solely to Brit-Art heavyweight Damien Hirst – for the first time. Arken also has a good café overlooking the sea. To get there, take the S-tog to Ishø (direction Hundige or Køge, 20 mins), and then bus No. 128; or the signposted walk takes 30–40 minutes.

DIRECTORY

A user-friendly alphabetical listing of practical information, plus hand-picked hotels and restaurants, clearly organised by area, to suit all budgets and tastes.

A

AGE RESTRICTIONS

In Denmark, you must be 18 to purchase alcohol and drink in a bar, and 16 to buy alcohol from a shop. The minimum age for driving is 18.

B

BUSINESS HOURS

Shops: Mon–Thur 9.30/10am–5.30pm, Fri 9.30/10am–6/7pm; Sat 9.30/10am–noon/1–4pm; Sun noon–4pm (from 2012).

Museums are often open late one night a week and closed on Mondays. Some have longer opening hours on Wednesdays.

Banks are usually open Mon–Fri 9.30am–4pm; some until 6pm Thur. They are closed on public holidays. If you are looking to exchange money out of usual hours, **Den Danske Bank** at Copenhagen airport is open 6am–8.30pm and **Forex** at Hovedbånegard is open 8am–9pm.

Office hours are usually Mon–Fri 9am–4/4.30pm.

C

CLIMATE

Copenhagen is on the same latitude as Moscow and Edinburgh. The winter months, December–February, are cold and windy and there are only five hours of daylight. January is the coldest month with an average daytime temperature of 1.9°C (35°F), July the warmest at 20.4°C (69°F). In summer there are between 16 and 18 hours of daylight on a clear day.

CRIME AND SAFETY

Copenhagen is one of the least dangerous places you could visit. However, it's never a bad thing to secure your personal possessions and not to take any personal risks. If you are victim of a crime, the police are very efficient and if there are witnesses, ask for help. **Main police station:** Politigården, tel: 33 14 14 48 or tel: 114

CUSTOMS REGULATIONS

Visitors arriving from EU countries can bring in 800 cigarettes (or 400 cigarillos or 200 cigars or 1kg of tobacco) and 10l of spirits (or 20l of fortified wine or 90l of table wine or 110l of beer). Visitors arriving from outside the EU can bring in 200 cigarettes (or 100 cigarillos, 50 cigars or 250g of tobacco) and 1l of spirits (or 2l of fortified wine or 4l of table wine or 16l of beer).

Food articles that are not vacuum-packed by the manufacturer cannot be brought into Denmark. Items with a value of more than 3,250dkk are subject to customs duty. If you are taking money (of any currency) worth over 10,000 euros in or out of the country, you must fill out a customs form.

Non-EU visitors travelling to a non-

Child-friendly City
Copenhagen is peaceful and safe, with plenty of sights and activities to keep kids amused. Most museums have excellent children's sections, and generally don't charge for under-18s; other attractions offer reduced rates. Highchairs and child-sized portions are widely available in cafés and restaurants. The local transport network in Copenhagen allows two children aged under 12 to travel free with each paying adult.

EU country are eligible for tax refunds: if you have spent over 300dkk in a single shop, ask the cashier for a tax-free form and get it stamped by customs on leaving the country. **Tax Free Worldwide** (www.taxfreeworldwide.com) or **Global Blue** (www.global-blue.com), who have desks in the airport, will refund around 20 percent of the purchase price.

D

DISABLED TRAVELLERS

The Danes are generally very thoughtful about customers' needs but not all hotels are suitable for disabled travellers. Contact the Tourist Board, **Wonderful Copenhagen**, for information on hotels, transport, museums and attractions.

For wheelchair users travelling by regional train (including the airport) contact the **DSB Handicap service**. All metro stations have lifts and most buses have collapsible ramps for the middle doors and a call button. Many cinemas and theatres have hearing loops; make sure to call venues for details. Most taxis offer specialised transport, but book ahead; one of the largest companies is **Taxa4x35**.

Taxa4x35: tel: 35 59 35 35; www.taxa.dk
DSB Handicap Service: tel: 70 13 14 15, then press '6'; www.dsb.dk
Wonderful Copenhagen: www.visit copenhagen.com; see also www.visit denmark.com (look for 'disabled travel' in the 'Denmark A–Z' section)

E

ELECTRICITY

220 volts AC (50 Hz) is the Danish standard. If you are travelling with electrical or electronic devices be sure to bring a two-pin continental adapter with you.

EMBASSIES AND CONSULATES

Australia: Dampfærgevej 26, 2nd Floor; tel: 70 26 36 76
Canada: Kristen Bernikowsgade 1; tel: 33 48 32 00
UK: Kastelsvej 36/38/40; tel: 35 44 52 00
USA: Dag Hammarskjölds Allé 24; tel: 33 41 71 00
For more information on embassies, visit www.embassyworld.com

EMERGENCY NUMBERS

Emergency services: 112
Airport police: 32 45 14 48
Politivagten (local police): 114 or 33 14 14 48
Doctor on call: 70 13 00 41
Emergency dentist: 35 38 02 51

G

GAY TRAVELLERS

Denmark doesn't bat an eyelid about gays and lesbians – it was the first country to recognise same-sex marriages. For advice and information,

contact **LGBT Denmark** (tel: 33 13 19 48; www.lbl.dk). *Out & About* magazine (www.outandabout.dk) features listings for bars, nightlife and events, including Copenhagen Pride (www.copenhagen pride.dk) in mid-August.

GREEN ISSUES

Copenhagen aims to become the world's greenest city by 2015. Organic goods are everywhere; the harbour is clean enough to swim in; low-pollution buses drive the streets; and just about everyone has a well-used bike. Between May and mid-November, the city operates a free bicycle scheme *(see p.106)*.

Carbon Offsetting: Air travel produces a huge amount of carbon dioxide and is a significant contributor to global warming. To offset the damage caused to the environment by your flight, visit www.climatecare.org or www.carbon neutral.com in the UK; or www.climate friendly.com or www.sustainable travelinternational.org in the US.

Gay Travel Agency
Set up in 2006, Pink Viking is Denmark's first tour operator to offer inbound and outbound trips for gay and lesbian clients wishing to visit Scandinavia. For more information contact Pink Viking; tel: +45 61 79 74 65; www.pinkviking.net

H

HEALTH

The Danish medical system will assist anyone in an emergency; however you should take out travel insurance before you leave. British nationals should take a European Health Insurance Card (EHIC; www.ehic.org.uk). Emergency hospital treatment is free, as long as you have not travelled to Denmark intending to receive treatment and are too ill to return home. Payment to pharmacies, doctors and dentists must be paid in full at the time of treatment: refunds are obtainable from the nearest municipal or health insurance office before leaving Denmark.

Prescription drugs for personal use (30 days' worth for Schengen residents, 15 days' worth for non-Schengen visitors) may be brought to Denmark: try to bring along your doctor's prescription too. Pharmacies are designated by a green 'A' for Apotek. Credit cards are not accepted in pharmacies. Full payment is required for all medications.

Late-night opening: Steno Apotek (24 hours); Vesterbrogade 6C (opposite main station); tel: 33 14 82 66

L

LOST PROPERTY

For items lost on the bus, go to www.moviatrafik.dk, click 'Kontakt', then 'Hittegods', then type in the bus number to find the correct contact telephone number. For items lost on the local (S) train, tel: 36 14 17 01. For lost luggage at the airport, tel: 32 47 47 25. For all other losses, ring the police station at Slotsherrensvej 113; tel: 38 74 88 22.

M

MAPS

The tourist board and most hotels offer free city maps with sights marked

Above from far left: celebrating at the Copenhagen Pride; meet the Danes; Copenhagen on the map; Thotts Palace houses the French Embassy.

on them. Some also show bus routes. These are fine for sightseeing. If you need a street index, the Insight Copenhagen Fleximap is a good option.

MEDIA

Newspapers: English-language newspapers are widely available, as are fashion and lifestyle magazines. The English-language weekly *Copenhagen Post* (www.cphpost.dk; free from tourist offices and some hotels) has local news and listings. Denmark's main newspapers are *Berlingske Tidende*, *Ekstra Bladet*, *Jyllands-Posten* and *Politiken*.

Television: Cable and satellite television is widely available. Foreign films are rarely dubbed into Danish and appear in the original version with subtitles.

MONEY

Cash machines: ATMs are open 24 hours and can usually be found outside banks and metro stations.

Credit cards: Visa, Mastercard and American Express are widely accepted but usually attract a fee. Many smaller, independent retailers (including pharmacies) do not accept them, so do not rely wholly on plastic.

Currency: Denmark uses Danish kroner (dkk). Danish notes come in 1,000dkk, 500dkk, 200dkk, 100dkk and 50dkk. Coins are in denominations of 20dkk, 10dkk, 5dkk 2dkk, 1dkk, and 50 øre (half a krone).

P

POST

Post offices usually open Mon–Fri 9/10am–5/6pm, Sat (if open) 9/10am–noon. The post office at Hovedbanegård (Central Station) has longer opening hours. 'A Prioritaire' mail is the fastest international option.

Hovedbanegård: Mon–Fri 8am–9pm, Sat–Sun 10am–4pm; www.postdanmark.dk.

R

RELIGION

Denmark's Constitution provides for freedom of religion. The evangelical Lutheran church is the State church. Officially, 80 percent of Danes are members, but church attendance is low and many Danes are agnostic or atheist. Muslims make up the second largest religious community (four percent of the population).

Places of Worship
Catholic: Skt Ansgars Kirke, Bredgade 64; tel: 33 13 37 62; www.sanktansgar.dk.
Church of England: St Albans, Churchillparken 11, Langelinie; tel: 39 62 77 36; www.st-albans.dk.
Jewish: Copenhagen Synagogue, Krystalgade 12, tel: 33 12 88 68; www.mosaiske.dk.
Muslim: Islamic Cultural Centre, Horsebakken 2; tel: 38 80 03 86.

Budget Copenhagen Much of Copenhagen is accessible on foot, parks are free, many museums offer free entry one day per week, and there are often free entertainments – check what's on at the tourist office. A free city tour leaves at 11am from the Rådhus steps. The National Theatre (already much subsidised) sells reduced unsold tickets on the day from 4pm.

TELEPHONES

Local Danish numbers have eight digits. There are no area codes.

International directory assistance: 113
International calls from Denmark: 00 + country code + area code + personal number
International calls to Denmark: 00 + 45 + personal number
International country codes: Britain +44, France +33, Germany +49, Ireland +353, Italy +39, Japan +81, Norway +47, Sweden +46, USA +1

Public telephones: Most public telephones take pre-paid cards, available from kiosks, supermarkets and petrol stations; some take credit cards and coins (but not 50 øre coins). No change is given. Collect calls to the US are not possible.

Mobile telephones: Danish mobile phones operate on the 900/1800 Mhz GSM network, on which most unlocked European phones will work. US visitors will only be able to use their cellphone in Denmark if it is a tri-band phone that can switch bands.

TIME ZONES

Denmark is one hour ahead of GMT. Summer time, when the clocks go forward one hour, runs from the last Sunday in March to the last Sunday in October.

Religious Harmony
Denmark has a long history of welcoming religious minorities and affording them equal treatment, although a recent increase in the Muslim population has led to some tensions. However, there is some question over whether these relate to religion or differences in language and ethnicity. The integration of immigrant groups from Islamic countries has become an important political and social topic of discussion.

TOURIST INFORMATION

The Wonderful Copenhagen tourist office is opposite the Tivoli entrance. You can get brochures, book hotels, drink coffee etc. Everyone speaks English. For a free tourist-information phone app, search iTunes or Android Market for 'Visitcopenhagen'.

Wonderful Copenhagen Tourist Information: Vesterbrogade 4A; tel: 70 22 24 42; www.visitcopenhagen.com; www.visitdenmark.dk; ispot.wonderful copenhagen.dk; July–Aug Mon–Sat 9am–8pm, Sun 10am–6pm; May–June Mon–Sat 9am–6pm, Sun 10am–2pm; Sept–Apr Mon–Fri 9am–4pm, Sat 9am–2pm.

Listings: The English newspaper the *Copenhagen Post* (published on Fridays) has a useful weekly guide to what's on.

TRANSPORT

Getting to Copenhagen is easy, with many airlines offering daily flights, as well as direct rail services from Sweden and Germany. Access from the airport is also very straightforward with train, bus and taxi options, which will take you to the city centre. Prices were correct at the time of going to press. There are also ferry services to Copenhagen (see p.105).

Getting There

By plane: Budget airlines offering flights to Copenhagen include EasyJet (www.easyjet.com) and Norwegian (www.norwegian.no). Copenhagen Air-

Above from far left: post box; tourist information is readily available; the main religion is Lutheran.

port, Kastrup (www.cph.dk) lies 12km (7.5 miles) east of the city centre, on Amager Island. There are trains to Hovedbanegård, Copenhagen's Central Station; and the Metro runs roughly every four minutes into the city centre. Both leave from Terminal 3 (where all passengers go for baggage reclaim and customs), take about 14 minutes and cost about 36dkk.

There is a **taxi rank** at Terminal 3. A taxi to the centre will cost between about 250–350dkk depending on the time and includes VAT and tip.

By train: There are six trains daily to/from Hamburg, Germany; and trains run every 10 minutes to/from Sweden, arriving at Hovedbanegård (Central Station). The S-tog (local) trains also leave from the Central Station and run on a separate network.

For German rail enquiries and bookings, contact **DB Bahn**: tel: +49 1805 996 633 (International); +44 8718 808 066 (UK); www.bahn.de.

For Swedish rail journeys, contact **SJ**: tel: +46 771 757 575; www.sj.se.

For Danish and outgoing international rail enquiries and bookings, contact **Danish Rail** (DSB): tel: 70 13 14 15; www.dsb.dk.

By bus: The biggest operator of scheduled coach services to/from Denmark is Eurolines: tel: +45 70 10 00 30 (Denmark), +44 8717 818 181 (UK); www.eurolines-travel.com. Buses stop at Copenhagen's Central Station.

By ferry: The new ferry terminal (www.cphport.dk), close to Nordhavn train station, is linked to the city centre by shuttle bus. **DFDS Seaways** (Denmark tel: +45 33 42 30 10; UK tel: 0871 522 9955; www.dfdsseaways.com) operate ferries from Oslo (16 hours) to Copenhagen and the UK (Harwich, 19 hours) to Esbjerg on Jutland three hours' drive away. Ferries from Germany with **Scandlines** (Denmark tel: + 45 33 15 15 15; Germany tel: +49 (0)381/5435-0; www.scandlines.com) arrive at Rødby, Rønne and Gedser.

By car: To get to Copenhagen, drivers arriving by ferry to Esbjerg from the UK (Harwich) should take the E20. Drivers arriving in Rødby from Germany (Puttgarden) should take the E47.

Both the Storebælt bridge/tunnel from Funen to Sjælland, and the Øresund bridge from Malmö to Copenhagen levy a toll.

Getting Around

Local transport tickets: For fare purposes, the city is divided into zones. Fares are charged on the number of zones that you pass through (minimum two).

The bus, harbour bus, metro and S-tog (local train) all use the same tickets so you can change between them without buying a new one. The cheapest option are to buy a discount Klippekort of 10 tickets (which can be shared between several people) or a 24-hour ticket. Alternatively, if you have a Copenhagen Card *(see p.107)*, local travel is free.

Tickets can be bought on the bus, at

Smoking
Smoking has been banned in public indoor places and private businesses since 2007, including restaurants, pubs, shops, public transport, entertainment venues and workplaces, although food-free bars smaller than 40 sq m/430 sq ft are exempt.

ticket offices or vending machines. Discount cards, with an average saving of 40 percent cannot be bought on the bus.

Individual tickets have a time limit of an hour for two zones (adult 24dkk/under 16s 12dkk) and you must clip your ticket when you get on the bus or on the train platform before you get on.

Using the night bus or the metro between 1am and 5am costs double the daytime fare.

By bus: Buses are operated by Movia (www.moviatrafik.dk). They are regular, although the city is so compact that it's usually easier to walk. Nearly all stop at either Rådhuspladsen or Hovedbanegård (Central Station).

Buses run daily between 5am and 12.30am and there are additional night buses from Rådhuspladsen (City Hall Square) to the suburbs.

Buses are yellow and you get on at the front and off at the back.

By S-tog: The S-tog (local train) connects Copenhagen with other towns on Sjælland. Tickets are available at all S-tog stations; travel is free on the first Sunday of the month.

By metro: The award-winning driverless metro (tel: 70 15 16 15; www.m.dk) operates a frequent service: every 4–6 minutes in the daytime, and every 15–20 minutes through the night. Currently there are two lines, M1 runs from Vanløse Station to Ørestad in West Amager, and M2 runs from Vanløse Station to Copenhagen Airport in East Amager. Both lines take you through the heart of the city.

The ambitious Cityringen circle extension, which will create two new lines and 17 new stations, is due to open in 2018.

Metro customer service: tel: 70 15 16 15 (Mon–Fri 8am–4pm); www.m.dk.

By bicycle: The Danes are avid cyclists and bicycles enjoy equal status with cars on Copenhagen's roads. When using the cycleways, keep to the right. Helmets are optional, but cycling without lights at night, under the influence of alcohol or jumping red lights can earn you an instant 500dkk fine.

From May to mid-November, you can join in for free by borrowing one of Copenhagen's **City Bikes** (www.bycyklen.dk), available at 125 stands around the inner city. Cyclists put a (refundable) 20-dkk coin into a slot to unlock a bike, and can keep it for as long as they like. The bikes may only be used within the old ramparts of the city, but this is where the sights are. The tourist office can provide you with a map.

Bike rental varies from 75–150dkk per day; 270–530dkk per week. Hotels and hostels frequently have bicycles for hire; otherwise try:

Baisikeli, Turesensgade 10; tel: 26 70 02 29; daily 10am–6pm; www.cph-bike-rental.dk. Uses its profits to ship 1200 bicycles per year to Africa.

Biking Copenhagen (bike tours); tel: 29 89 93 73; www.bikingcopenhagen.com

Kobenhavns Cykelbørs, Gothersgade 157; tel: 33 14 07 17; Mon–Fri

Tour Operators
Tour operators in Copenhagen offer myriad bus, boat and bike rides, ghost walks, architecture tours, Segway trips, jaunts for joggers, and even a walk that focuses on how the city smelled 200 years ago! Contact Wonderful Copenhagen for more information.

Above from far left: boats waiting for tourists; SAS, the Scandinavian airline.

9am–5.30pm; Sat 10am–1.30pm; www.cykelboersen.dk

Harbour buses: The blue-and-yellow harbour buses follow two routes. The 991/992 sails from Nordre Toldbod (near the Little Mermaid) to Tegl-holmen, in the southwest, stopping at the Black Diamond, Knippel's Bridge (Christianshavn), Nyhavn and the Opera House. The 993 zips between Nyhavn and the Opera House. Harbour buses run daily from 6am–6/7pm, and accept local transport tickets. They are free with the Copenhagen Card.

By car: Cars are not practical in Copenhagen, but if you do hire a car, you must be over 20 years old and hold a valid licence. Some car firms may stipulate that you have to be over 25.

Danes drive on the right and speed limits are 110 or 130 kmh (66 or 80 mph) on motorways, 80 kmh (50 mph) on other roads and 50 kmh (30 mph) in a built-up area. Take a UK or EU driving licence and a warning tri-angle, and wear a seat belt at all times.

Headlights must be dipped at all times. Be aware of cycle lanes on both sides of the road in towns. *Parkering Forbudt* means No Parking.

Car hire companies
Budget: tel: 33 55 05 00, www.budget. dk
Sixt: tel: 32 48 11 00, dk.sixt.com

By taxi and rickshaw: Taxis can be identified by the sign on the roof with the word FRI, meaning 'free'. Most drivers speak English and often some German. They can give you receipts and you can pay with a credit card. The basic fare for a taxi is 24dkk, then 13.80dkk for each km thereafter Mon–Fri 7am–4pm; 17.40dkk per km Fri–Sat 11pm–7am and 14.80dkk per km at all other times. Tips are not expected, but it is usual to round up the final amount.

Cycle rickshaws are also available for short rides around town and can be found at Storkspringvandet, Nyhavn, Tivoli and Rådhuspladsen. Prices vary so negotiate first.

Amager Øbro taxi: tel: 32 51 51 51
Copenhagen Rickshaw: tel: 35 43 01 22; www.rickshaw.dk
Dantaxi: tel: 70 25 25 25
Taxa 4x35: tel: 70 25 25 25
Minibuses/handicap: tel: 35 39 35 35

VISAS

Citizens of the EU do not need a visa; other visitors should check with their country. Visitors not obliged to have a visa are allowed to stay in Denmark for up to 90 days. Foreign nationals are usually required to have a work and residence permit as a prerequisite to seeking paid or unpaid work in Denmark. See www.nyidanmark.dk.

WEIGHTS AND MEASURES

The metric system is used in Denmark.

Copenhagen Card
A Copenhagen Card (CPH Card) gives entry to 65 attractions in the Copenhagen area, offers some discounts and also entitles you to free travel on trains, buses and the Metro. They are valid for 24 hours (229dkk for adults/ 115dkk for children aged 10–15) or 72 hours (459dkk/ 225dkk). Up to two children under the age of 10 are allowed free with each adult card. You can buy them online or at the tourist office, airport and main railway stations.

ACCOMMODATION

Tivoli and Radhuspládsen

Cabinn City

Mitchellsgade 14; tel: 33 46
16 16; www.cabinn.dk; S-tog:
Hovedbanegård; €

There are three of these attractive,
functional budget hotels in Copenhagen *(see p.113 for the other two)*, with
modern Danish decor. Space is limited
(many rooms have bunk beds – think
of a ship's cabin, hence 'cabinn') but
this particular hotel is superbly situated, just a short walk from buzzing
Tivoli. The all-inclusive breakfasts
(60dkk) are healthy, copious and good
value. A good option for families and
anyone not expecting to do much more
than sleep here.

Danhostel Copenhagen City

H.C. Andersens Boulevard 50;
tel: 33 11 85 85; www.danhostel.dk/
copenhagencity; bus: 5A; €

A five-star youth hostel with a great
location right in the centre of town and
far-reaching views. It's modern, comfortable and has plenty of family rooms
(accommodating up to 6 people), which
are extremely good value if you fill them
up. You will need an international YHA
card but the investment is covered by the
saving on the cost of a bed.

First Hotel Kong Frederik

Vester Voldgade 25; tel: 33 12 59
02; www.firsthotels.com; bus: 6a;
€€€€

The history of this site as a hotel and
inn dates back to the 14th century. Situated close to Rådhuspladsen and
Tivoli, the hotel was completely ren-

ovated in 2010. Public areas have
retained the hotel's classic 'English'
atmosphere, while bedrooms are more
Scandinavian, done out in a dusky
palette of blacks, greys and creams.
Rooms can get rather warm in
summer.

Hotel Alexandra

H.C. Andersens Boulevard 8; tel: 33
74 44 44; www.hotelalexandra.dk;
bus: 6A; €€€€

Formerly an apartment block dating
from the 1880s, this retro hotel with
good environmental credentials has
been in business since 1910. It is
stylishly decorated with plenty of
design classics from the 1940s and 50s,
from Arne Jacobsen furniture (see
room 223 in particular) to Kaare Klint
chairs and Poul Henningsen lighting.
It's definitely worth paying extra to
stay in one of the 13 'Danish Design'
rooms, each furnished in tribute to a
particular designer.

Hotel Danmark

Vester Voldgade 89; tel: 33 11 48 06;
www.hotel-danmark.dk; bus: 10; €€

Located next to Rådhuspladsen, this
modern, bright hotel offers rooms
tastefully furnished in subdued Scan-

Price for a standard double room for one night without breakfast in high season:	
€€€€	over 1,600dkk
€€€	1,400–1,600dkk
€€	1,000–1,400dkk
€	under 1,000dkk

dinavian style. Clean, central, cheap and carbon-neutral.

Hotel Fox
Jarmers Plads 3; tel: 33 13 30 00; www.hotelfox.dk; bus: 5a, 6a; €€–€€€

A short walk from Rådhuspladsen, this is definitely one of Copenhagen's most extreme hotels – it's either your cup of tea, or it isn't. All the rooms have been individually designed by 21 international artists and vary from startling white to one decorated like a children's fairytale forest. Visit rooms online before you check in as you can't change rooms once you get there; also note, though, that while the hotel will do its best to give you the room you want, there are no guarantees. The bar and restaurant downstairs are good.

Imperial Hotel
Vester Farimagsgade 9; tel: 33 12 80 00; www.imperialhotel.dk; €€€

A good location next to Vesterport Station and a few minutes' walk from Rådhuspladsen and Tivoli Gardens, this modern, stylish hotel is far more prepossessing on the inside than on the outside, with well-appointed, elegant rooms, as well as fine restaurants and on-site parking.

Nimb
Tivoli, Bernstorffsgade 5; tel: 88 70 00 00; www.tivoli.dk; S-tog: Hovedbanegård; €€€€

A romantic's dream, Nimb is located in a fairylit Moorish palace inside Tivoli gardens. Its 13 fabulous boutique rooms contain a deeply satisfying blend of modern and antique furniture, and sleek bathrooms come with bathtubs and double sinks. Working fireplaces add to the romance in winter. Brunch is served until 2pm, and the hotel's restaurant is the Michelin-starred Herman. Entry to Tivoli is included in the price.

Radisson Blu Royal Hotel
Hammerichsgade 1; tel: 33 42 60 00; www.radissonsas.com; S-tog: Vesterport, Hovedbanegård; €€€–€€€€

This is Copenhagen's most iconic hotel; designed, down to the cutlery and the door knobs, by the famous architect and designer, Arne Jacobsen. Although only one room (606) retains its original decor, this hotel is still popular with the rich and famous and has a nice retro/modern feel. There is also a popular restaurant, Alberto K, on the top floor, with fabulous views over Tivoli Gardens and the city. There is also a sauna and private parking. Rates are generally lower at weekends and the family rooms can be quite reasonable if there are four of you.

Scandic Copenhagen
Vester Søgade 6; tel: 33 14 35 35; www.scandichotels.com; €€€

A comfortable, centrally placed, skyscraper hotel that looks out over Copenhagen's reservoirs and the Tycho Brahe Planetarium: all rooms come with a pair of binoculars so that you can admire the view. The Scandic Copenhagen is popular with both business and leisure travellers,

Above from far left: every room is a feast for the eyes at Hotel Fox.

Where to Stay
Many hotels are near Hovebanegård (Central Station), the cheaper ones are around the Vesterbro area and the more expensive ones around Rådhuspladsen, within a short walk of the city's main sights. There are also several smart hotels around Kongens Nytorv and Nyhavn, but don't always expect a view. A little bit out of the way, but with good views, are the new hotels on Kalvebod Brygge, south of Slotsholmen. Alternatively, head away from the tourist centre and stay near Rosenborg or Amalienborg. Copenhagen's transport is so good that nowhere is far from the city centre.

Breakfast

Many hotels include breakfast with the room; always ask as otherwise it usually costs between 1,000 and 1,700dkk. This may seem a lot but a coffee and pastry will set you back 600–700dkk in a café, so a hearty breakfast of all you can eat may well be a good investment.

including families. At the time of writing it was undergoing a major renovation, due to be completed in May 2012: expect shining new rooms, a gym, lobby, restaurant and lounge bar.

Scandic Palace Hotel

Rådhuspladsen 57; tel: 33 14 40 50; www.scandichotels.dk; bus: all Rådhuspladsen buses; €€€–€€€€

An imposing historical landmark on Rådhuspladsen with its own rival clocktower. Newly renovated in 2008, the public areas thankfully retain their old-world, Victorian grandeur while the comfortable bedrooms, which are all a good size, especially for Copenhagen, have been stylishly redesigned using a modern idiom.

Wakeup Copenhagen

Carsten Niebuhrs Gade 11; tel: 44 80 00 00; www.wakeupcopenhagen. com; S-tog: Hovedbanegård; €€

Wakeup Copenhagen, a budget hotel designed by Kim Utzon, is well priced and a mere ten-minute walk from the railway station. Rooms are small, sharp, and crispy clean, with flatscreen TVs and free wifi. Prices rise as you go higher up the building – the 'Wakeup Heaven' rooms on the top floor have the best views – but there is a discount for online bookings.

Zleep Hotel Astoria

Banegårdspladsen 4; tel: 70 23 56 35; www.zleephotels.com; S-tog: Hovedbanegård; €

This old railway hotel dating from the 1930s has been renovated, keeping ele-

ments of the 1930s original (including the revolving doors at the entrance, the first in Denmark), while updating the rooms to suit more modern tastes and requirements. The rooms are designed in black and white with shades of grey and purple as contrasting colours and the furniture is modern. Book well in advance for reduced rates.

Strøget and Around
Ascot Hotel

Studiestræde 61; tel: 33 12 60 00; www.ascot-hotel.dk; €€€€

Set in a distinguished old bathhouse building in the Latin Quarter, this hotel, offers suites, some with kitchenettes if you are into a bit of self-catering. Rooms, decorated with a mixture of antique and modern furniture, are a hit-and-miss affair. Some are fresh and stylish, while others need a makeover; but on the plus side, it's very central and you won't be bothered by traffic.

First Hotel Sankt Petri

Krystalgade 22; tel: 33 45 91 00; www.hotelsktpetri.com; €€€€

This upmarket, modern five-star hotel is located in the ancient centre of the town. 'Bespoke' is a word that applies to virtually everything here; from the

Price for a standard double room for one night without breakfast in high season:

€€€€	over 1,600dkk
€€€	1,400–1,600dkk
€€	1,000–1,400dkk
€	under 1,000dkk

original artworks on the walls to the orchids and designer modern decor. The bathrooms are stunning. There is a good restaurant, a couple of excellent bars and a pretty atrium where live jazz is played and international DJs spin their discs. In summer, there is also an attractive outdoor area for drinks and dinner.

Hotel Kong Arthur

Nørre Søgade 11; tel: 33 11 12 12; www.kongarthur.dk; S-Tog: Nørreport; €€€

Established in 1882 and situated slightly off the beaten track beside Peblinge Sø, this hotel has retained much of its original charm with attractive rooms and a pretty, conservatory-type inner courtyard. It is a popular choice with both Danish and foreign visitors and has a friendly and very Danish atmosphere. Some of the suites have jacuzzis. Treatments are available from the excellent spa located in the hotel.

Hotel 27

Løngangstræde 27; tel: 70 27 56 27; www.hotel27.dk; bus: 10; €€–€€€

Stylishly decorated to Danish taste using a palette of red, black and white, this is a reasonably priced 'life style' hotel in the centre of town, also home to the Icebar, a bar entirely made of ice. The light evening buffet saves on restaurant costs.

Ibsens Hotel

Vendersgade 23; tel: 33 13 19 13; www.ibsenshotel.dk; S-Tog:

Nørreport; €€

In the same group as the Hotel Kong Arthur and Hotel Fox, this is a pleasant, comfortable three-star hotel, although it won't win awards for striking decor. Located near Peblinge Sø, a five-minute walk from Nørreport station. It's also possible to hire an electric car here.

Kongens Nytorv and Nyhavn

Best Western Hotel City

Peder Skramsgade 24; tel: 33 13 06 66; www.hotelcity.dk; €€

Located in an elegant town house, the City has an international feel, clearly expressed in its striking modern decor. It has a hospitable and friendly atmosphere – nothing is too much trouble for the staff – and does a good breakfast buffet.

Copenhagen Strand

Havnegade 37; tel: 33 48 99 00; www.copenhagenstrand.dk; €€€–€€€€

This cosy three-star hotel can be found on a side street just off Nyhavn in a converted warehouse dating from 1869. Its decor is slightly rustic yet modern and brings to mind its maritime position and history.

Hotel d'Angleterre

Kongens Nytorv 34; tel: 33 12 00 95; www.remmen.dk; S-tog: Kongens Nytorv; €€€€

The Hotel d'Angleterre has been closed for a mighty overhaul, and is due to reopen in 2012 as a 'fairytale' hotel. Traditionally it has always provided a

Early Booking
Early bookings are usually cheaper than the official rack rates; web bookings are often cheaper still and some hotels have special deals. However, it is always worth ringing up to find out if a hotel (even the expensive ones) can give you an even better deal; they may be able to if business is slow.

refuge for the wealthy, the important and the beautiful: it is the place for formal elegance and the only hotel in Copenhagen where you will find a Victorian palm court. Facilities include an upmarket restaurant and a spa and fitness centre with a heated pool.

Hotel Opera
Tordenskjoldsgade 15; tel: 33 47 83 00; www.hotelopera.dk; €€€
This is another charming three-star hotel belonging to the Arp-Hansen group. Located on a side street close to the Royal Theatre on Kongens Nytorv, this English-inspired hotel dates from 1869. Rooms are comfortable but vary in size, as do the beds.

71 Nyhavn Hotel
Nyhavn 71; tel: 33 43 62 00; www.71nyhavnhotel.com; €€€
This pleasant hotel overlooking the harbour is housed in two former warehouses on Nyhavn, which were once used to store spices from the Far East. The atmosphere is one of upmarket rusticity and many original features remain. The rooms are full of character but are tiny; some have harbour views. The restaurant is recommended.

The Royal District

Adina Apartment Hotel
Amerika Plads 7; tel: 39 69 10 00; www.adina.eu; bus: 26; €€€–€€€€
Just north of the Little Mermaid, this hotel is a little distance out of the centre. However, it's very handy for anyone about to board a cruise ship leaving from Copenhagen's new port.

It consistently gets positive reviews from its guests for its splendid air-conditioned apartments, with bedroom, lounge, kitchenette and balcony. Facilities include a gym and small pool.

Copenhagen Admiral Hotel
Toldodgade 24–8; tel: 33 74 14 14; www.admiralhotel.dk; €€€–€€€€
A stone's throw from Nyhavn, this fabulous warehouse conversion (formerly a granary) is full of original beams and a modern rustic stance with designer teak furniture; every room is different. Outside iron canons salute you as you pass into the enormous galley-like lobby with naval memorabilia and some lovely model ships on view. It features its own, very good restaurant, SALT, and a sauna and steam bath facility on the top floor.

Phoenix Copenhagen
Bredgade 37; tel: 33 95 95 00; www.phoenixcopenhagen.dk; bus: 1a, 15, 19; €€€
This is an elegant hotel in a 17th-century mansion, close to the Royal Palace and Kongens Nytorv. All rooms and suites are air-conditioned and furnished in the French Louis XVI style, although some are starting to look a little frayed at the edges.

Price for a standard double room for one night without breakfast in high season:

€€€€	over 1,600dkk
€€€	1,400–1,600dkk
€€	1,000–1,400dkk
€	under 1,000dkk

Scandic Front Hotel

Skt Annæ Plads 21; tel: 33 13 34 00; www.scandichotels.com; €€€€

This is a stylish, modern boutique hotel set in a quiet location not far from Nyhavn. Kids are welcome and some rooms have a stunning harbour view of the Opera House. The split-level suites come with top-of-the-range coffee-making machines.

Rosenborg and Around

Hotel Christian IV

Dronningens Tværgade 45; tel: 33 32 10 44; www.hotelchristianiv.dk; €€

A small, pleasant hotel located beside the lovely King's Garden (Kongens Have). Rooms are neat and bright, and fitted with modern Danish furniture; some quieter rooms overlook the inner courtyard. Guests have free entry to the gym round the corner on Adelgade (www.fitnessdk.dk). Complimentary coffee, tea, fruit and cake available.

Vesterbro and Frederiksberg

Absalon Hotel

Helgolandsgade 15; tel: 33 24 22 11; www.absalon-hotel.dk; €

If you're looking for value and a central location, this family-run place has both. Double rooms in the B&B annexe (with shared bathrooms) start from 650dkk; the main hotel has private bathrooms. Rooms are a mixed bag: some are sweet and homely, others a little old-fashioned.

Axel Guldsmeden

Helgolandsgade 11; tel: 33 31 32 66; www.hotelguldsmeden.dk; €€€–€€€€

This lovely place is one of three Guldsmeden hotels in Copenhagen; the company prides itself on its socially responsible, eco-friendly and organic credentials. All offer distinctive rooms decorated in colonial style – the furniture is made in Bali – as well as all mod-cons and delicious organic breakfasts. Axel's advantages over the other hotels in the group include four stars, a great central location, and a spa and sauna.

Bertrams Guldsmeden

Vesterbrogade 107; tel: 33 25 04 05; www.hotelguldsmeden.dk; bus: 6a; €€€

Carlton Guldsmeden

Vesterbrogade 66; tel: 33 22 15 00; www.hotelguldsmeden.dk; bus: 6a; €€

Both hotels belong to the same chain as the newer Axel Guldsmeden. They are both a bit further down Vesterbrogade, which is fine to walk but a bus or cab will be appealing if you have had a long day. Bertrams is particularly charming, with great service and a pleasant courtyard garden.

Cabinn Express

Danasvej 32–34, Frederiksberg; tel: 33 21 04 00; www.cabinn.dk; Metro: Forum; €

Cabinn Scandinavia

Vodroffsvej 55, Frederiksberg; tel: 35 36 11 11; www.cabinn.dk; Metro: Forum; €

Both of these hotels in the stylish and

Above from far left: stylish Scandic Front Hotel; do not disturb; the lobby in Front Hotel; the breakfast bar at the Axel Guldsmeden.

Renting an Apartment
If you're staying one week or longer, renting an apartment might be a more economical and practical option. Citilet Apartments (tel: 22 77 10 30; www.citilet.dk; citilet@citilet.dk) have some very luxurious lets right in the old town. Hay 4 You (Vimmelskaftet 49,1st floor; tel: 33 33 08 05; www.hay4you.dk) is an agency offering a variety of cosy local apartments.

popular budget chain are located close to Peblinge Sø (Lake), approximately a 12-minute walk from Rådhuspladsen. You can sleep a family of four for under 1,000dkk. *(See also Cabinn City, p.108.)*

Clarion Collection Hotel Mayfair
Helgolandsgade 3; tel: 70 12 17 00; www.choicehotels.dk; €€

This early 20th-century hotel is a wonderful choice. Each room is individually decorated, and the same sense of style and humour pervades the public areas too. With clean, fresh decor, a cosy atmosphere and good service. Look out for good-value packages online that include room, organic breakfast buffet and an evening meal.

Copenhagen Crown
Vesterbrogade 41; tel: 33 21 21 66; www.copenhagencrown.dk; bus: 6a; €

This fresh, modern hotel in the centre of things has amenities for business travellers as well as holidaymakers. Most of the rooms look onto an inner courtyard, so street noise is less of an issue here than in some other central hotels.

Copenhagen Island
Kalvebod Brygge 53; tel: 33 38 96 00; www.copenhagenisland.com; S-Tog: Dybbelsbro, bus: 11A; €€€

This stylish hotel is located on an artificial island in Copenhagen Harbour east of Vesterbro. It offers all the mod cons, including a lovely restaurant, fit-ness centre with views over the harbour and flat-screen TVs in all the rooms. Depending on dates, a standard double room can be under 1,000dkk.

First Hotel Vesterbro
Vesterbrogade 23–29; tel: 33 78 80 00; www.firsthotels.dk/vesterbro; bus: 6a; €€–€€€€

First Hotel is centrally placed on Vesterbrogade and its attractive minimalist decor retains a sense of warmth, thanks perhaps to the cherry-wood furniture. All the rooms are a decent size and look down onto an internal, airy atrium where you have breakfast. In days of yore, it used to be the local porn cinema. Recommended in its price range.

Grand Hotel
Vesterbrogade 9a; tel: 33 27 69 00; www.grandhotel.dk; bus: 6a; €€–€€€

An attractive facade, dating from 1890, fronts another tasteful hotel belonging to the Arp-Hansen group. It is centrally placed on a corner in uptown Vesterbro and was carefully modernized a few years ago in a manner that preserved much of its original character. Decor is in calming tones with splashes of accentuating colour.

Price for a standard double room for one night without breakfast in high season:

€€€€	over 1,600dkk
€€€	1,400–1,600dkk
€€	1,000–1,400dkk
€	under 1,000dkk

Hotel Avenue

Åboulevard 29; tel: 35 37 31 11; www.avenuehotel.dk; Bus: 12, 66, 69, Metro: Forum; €€–€€€

On the very edge of Frederiksberg, tipping into Nørrebro, you'll find this funky little design hotel, with its cosy rooms and friendly staff. The lounge (a perfect example of Danish *hygge*) is perfect for relaxing with a glass of wine, and there's also a pleasing courtyard. The generous breakfast buffet includes homemade bread.

Hotel dgi-Byens

Tietgensgade 65; tel: 33 29 80 70; www.dgi-byen.com; €€

Close to Central Station, this hotel is comfortable but unspectacular; some rooms are a little shabby. It is popular with families, as it is just one street away from Tivoli and based inside a sports centre, which contains an excellent swimming complex, spa and bowling alley.

Marriott Copenhagen

Kalvebod Brygge 5; tel: 88 33 99 00; www.marriott.com/cphdk; bus: 30; €€€

This hotel offers a waterside location with a lovely view through the huge glass windows on the harbour side; comfortable, good-sized rooms; a health spa; and all the mod cons and perks that you would expect from a five-star hotel. The only drawback is that it is on a main road, which makes no difference when you are inside but makes getting places a little less straightforward on foot.

CPH Living

Langebrogade 1C; tel: 61 60 85 46; www.cphliving.com; Bus: 5A; €€–€€€

One of Copenhagen's most unusual hotels, you'll find CPH Living in the harbour just off Christianshavn. But this isn't some decrepit old boat forced to eke out its retirement as a hostel: this is a purpose-built floating hotel with a splendid design aesthetic. Style-savvy rooms have floor-to-ceiling windows so you can enjoy the harbour views; and in fine weather, there's a fabulous sun deck too.

Crowne Plaza Copenhagen Towers

Ørestads Boulevard 114–118; tel: 88 77 66 55; www.crowneplaza.com; €€€

Opened in 2010, this place has supersleek rooms and amazing views over Amager (especially at night). Careful environmental consideration went into its building – it contains Denmark's first groundwater-based heating system and the largest solar panels in Scandinavia. A free shuttle runs to the airport.

Hilton Copenhagen Airport Hotel

Ellehammersvej 20; tel: 32 50 15 01; www.hilton.com; €€–€€€€

Directly linked to Terminal 3, this award-winning five-star hotel is frequently voted Copenhagen's best hotel. It also has the largest rooms in the city and a spa and wellness centre.

Above from far left: the superb swimming pool at the Hilton Copenhagen Airport Hotel; many hotel rooms are a showcase for Danish design; the Hilton Copenhagen Airport Hotel; relaxing in style.

Construction Chaos

The metro system is currently undergoing a major extension, with 17 stations being built across the city centre from now until 2018. Naturally this involves a lot of construction noise (usually from 8am to 5pm) and road closures (which are affecting some bus routes). If you are staying centrally, check with your hotel if this is a concern.

Café Ultimo

Tivoli; tel: 33 75 07 51; lunch:
noon–4pm; dinner 5–10pm);
€€–€€€

This Italian restaurant, housed in a
pretty, white glass structure, is not far
from Tivoli's lake and dates from 1883.
It offers such delicacies as pan-fried
foie gras with pear chutney and rucola
tossed in truffle oil as well as a good
selection of pasta dishes and pizzas.

Grøften

Tivoli; tel: 33 75 06 75;
www.groeften.dk; noon–Tivoli
closing time; €€

A Tivoli stalwart since 1874, serving
traditional food to generations of
Danes. Come here for open sandwiches at lunchtime, or to sample its
speciality dish, a beetroot borsch. It's
big but cosy, and is run with smiling
efficiency and real kindness to kids.

Nimb

Berstorffsgade 5; tel: 88 70 00 00;
www.nimb.dk; €€€–€€€€

The wonderful Moorish Palace in Tivoli
has recently undergone an extensive
transformation, taking it back to the
original design of 1909. It is now a
gourmet heaven with a Michelin-
starred restaurant (€€€€) where chef
Thomas Herman takes Danish dishes
and reinterprets them in more modern
style. Three other top-rated restaurants
offer more informal dining: the family-
friendly brasserie (€€€), a Bar'n'Grill
(€€€), and the Terrace (€€€), a
French-inspired bistro.

Fiasco

Gammel Kongevej 176,
Frederiksberg; tel: 33 31 74 87;
Tue–Sat 5.30–10pm; €€

This rustic, unpretentious Italian restaurant offers borderline gourmet dishes
at very reasonable prices. In the
summer you can eat alfresco.

Formel B

Vesterbrogade 182, Vesterbro; tel:
33 25 10 66; www.formel-b.dk;
Mon–Sat 5.30pm–1am, last table
reservation at 10pm; €€€€

A charming Michelin-starred restaurant where you can relax in a restful
interior decorated in shades of white,
chocolate and taupe. The menu
changes every two weeks and offers
dishes such as Danish cod with water-
cress, dandelion and cod roe; monkfish
with snails, mushrooms and basil; and
escalope of foie gras with kale and
giblets. In summer, there's a terrace for
outdoor dining.

Mielcke & Hurtigkarl

Frederiksberg Runddel 1;
tel: 38 34 84 36; €€€€

This experimental gourmet place is
located in the beautiful rose gardens of
Frederiksberg Park. The intimate inte-

Prices for an average three-
course meal without wine:

€€€€	over 550dkk
€€€	400–550dkk
€€	250–400dkk
€	under 250dkk

Above from far left: relaxed atmosphere; the famous Danish pastries and bacon; refined dining.

rior is great for romantic dinners, but the terrace is the place to be on a fine day. The restaurant has its own herb garden which informs the ever-changing tasting menu.

Nose2Tail

Flæsketorvet 13A; tel: 33 93 50 45; Tue–Thur 5.30–midnight, Fri–Sat 5.30pm–1am; €€

Hidden in a vaulted, white-tiled cellar in Copenhagen's former butchers' district, Nose2Tail has an appropriately meaty menu (free-range and organic, naturally): think pork crackling, juicy sausages and lamb steaks. Large, shareable meat-and-cheese platters let you try bits of everything.

Paté Paté

Slagterboderne 1; tel: 39 69 55 57; Mon–Wed 8am–midnight, Thur 8am–1am, Fri 8am–3am, Sat 10am–3am, Sun 10am–midnight; €€

Cosy, candlelit Paté Paté is a sociable place to dine. Spanish and Moroccan dishes, including plates of tapas, are served at big tables which you share with other diners. You can stop by for a breakfast croissant, but with its bistro feel and huge winelist, it really comes into its own at night.

Restaurant Klubben

Enghavevej 4; tel: 33 31 40 15; €

This pub is a little too rough and ready to tempt many tourists if they are not already in the know. However, if you are happy on wobbly tables with plastic table cloths and occasional beery-looking locals, this place offers generous portions of traditional home cooking such as *frikadeller* with creamed cabbage and beetroot or the traditional Danish plate of herring.

The Latin Quarter, Strøget and Around

Det Lille Apotek

Store Kannikestræde 15; tel: 33 12 56 06; www.detlilleapotek.dk; daily 11.30am–midnight; €–€€

The 'Little Pharmacy' is Copenhagen's oldest cellar restaurant, with crooked walls and antiques. It claims many writers as former customers, including Hans Christian Andersen and Ludvig Holberg and serves hearty Danish fish and meat dishes. Students love it.

Frankie's Køkken

Admiralgade 25; tel: 33 13 33 77; www.bistrobooking.dk; Mon–Sat 5.30pm–midnight; €–€€

This cellar restaurant, on a quaint little street in the old town offers a small menu of French-style meat and fish mains (scallops, coq au vin, duck confit) served on charmingly mismatched plates by a cheery bunch of waiters.

Kobenhavner Kafeen

Badstuestræde 10; tel: 33 32 80 81; daily 11am–midnight; €–€€

This small restaurant has an old-time atmosphere and a traditional menu to go with it; *flæskesteg* (roasted pork, a Christmas speciality), *frikadeller* (meatballs), grilled plaice and a recommended cold table and daily 'Plate' of marinated salmon, herring, shrimp, meatballs, vegetables and baked bread for 198dkk.

Bådteatret

In summer, the theatre boat on Nyhavn is a more charming and usually less crowded spot than any of the bars on the north side. It offers experimental theatre performances downstairs but if your Danish isn't up to it, sitting on deck with a glass in your hand is a very enjoyable way to spend the evening. Prices are not above average either.

Marv & Ben

Snaregade 4; tel: 33 91 01 91; www.marvogben.dk; Mon–Sat 6–10pm; €€€

This fabulous Nordic gastropub takes a great deal of pride in producing succulent, flavour-packed dishes based on seasonal ingredients: duck breast with chestnuts and sorrel, haddock served with cockles and a smidgen of seaweed, or juicy slow-roasted pork.

Riz Raz

Kompanistræde 20; tel: 33 15 05 75; www.rizraz.dk; daily 11.30am–midnight; €

This attractive Mediterranean restaurant is very popular and offers an excellent and varied vegetarian buffet. The cuisines of Lebanon, Morocco and Italy are all inspirations. There are some meat dishes for the more carnivorous.

Kongens Nytorv, Nyhavn and Around

Custom House

Havnegade 44; tel: 33 31 01 30; www.customhouse.dk; Bacino: Mon–Fri 11.30am–2pm, Mon–Sat 6–10pm, €€–€€€; Bar and Grill: daily 11.30–2.30pm & 5–10pm; €€; Ebisu Tue–Sat 6.30–10.30pm; €€–€€€

Overlooking the harbour is this 'complex' of Conran eateries housed in a functionalist 'jazz-modern' style building. Choose between Bacino, offering traditional Italian fare in a creamy-white interior, a bar and grill offering hearty Danish-European dishes and Ebisu, a Japanese grill and sushi bar, where the tasting menus start from 499dkk. There are also two bars open until late.

Nyhavns Færgekro

Nyhavn 5; tel: 33 15 15 88; www.nyhavnsfærgekro.dk; daily 9am–1pm; €–€€

An unpretentious lunch restaurant set in an 18th-century building, serving particularly good traditional food, including *smørrebrød*, and a good herring buffet.

Restaurant Koefoed

Landgreven 3; tel: 56 48 22 24; www.restaurant-koefoed.dk; Mon–Sat noon–10pm; €€€

The classy, slow-food menu specialises in food from the Danish island of Bornholm. Diners are treated to fish prepared in Allinge's famous smokehouses, beer from the Svaneke brewery and Bornholm cheeses. Indecisive types can go for the five-course tasting menu.

Restaurant Pierre André

Ny Østergade 21; tel: 33 16 17 19; Tue–Sat noon–2.30pm and 6–10pm; €€–€€€

This is an intimate, bistro-style, yellow-walled restaurant offering delicious French food prepared by a genuine French chef. There's a small

---

Prices for an average three-course meal without wine:

€€€€	over 550dkk
€€€	400–550dkk
€€	250–400dkk
€	under 250dkk

but perfectly considered menu, and a laidback ambiance. Sit back and enjoy.

Umami

Store Kongensgade 59; tel: 33 38 75 00; www.restaurantumami.dk; Mon–Thur 6–10pm, Fri–Sat 6–11pm; €€€€

Cool and very expensive, this stylish Japanese-French fusion restaurant is a popular celebrity haunt. There is a ground-floor cocktail bar and a sushi bar and restaurant upstairs serving dishes such as ginger-poached duck breast with gyoza, sesame and garlic; grilled sea bream with mushrooms and artichoke and cauliflower purée, white soya sauce, chili and coriander; and grilled veal tenderloin with wasabi and truffle sauce.

Rosenborg and Around

Ankara

Krystalgade 8; tel: 33 15 19 15; www.restaurant-ankara.dk; Mon–Sat 1pm–midnight; €

Extensive Turkish buffet-style eaterie adapted for Danish tastes; a belly dancer provides the entertainment. In a city of expensive restaurants, the evening buffet here is a bargain.

Firefly

Frederiksborggade 26; tel: 33 36 33 30; daily from 10pm; €

Copenhagen's only 100 percent meat-free restaurant is located in pleasant café-style premises near the Botanical Gardens and offers a small menu of veggie burritos, tofu cutlets and curries. It also serves speciality teas, including one picked by monkeys!

Kokkeriet

Kronprinsessegade 64; tel: 33 15 27 77; www.kokkeriet.dk; Mon–Sat 6–9pm; €€€€

This charming, relaxed modern restaurant boasts one Michelin star and a six-course set menu offering beautifully presented, interesting food combinations: scallops in buttermilk, with cabbage and malt; foie gras giblets, apples and cowberry; and carrot ice cream with lychee and liquorice. You can also eat à la carte and arrange to take lessons from the chef!

Kong Hans Kælder

Vingaardsstræde 6; tel: 33 11 68 68; www.konghans.dk; Mon–Sat 6–10pm; €€€€

Set in Copenhagen's oldest building, this structure is mentioned in medieval texts. In the 19th century, Hans Christian Andersen lived in its garret. Now a Michelin-starred, expensive treat, it's one of the most splendid venues in the city. The food is French-influenced with an emphasis on simplicity and fresh ingredients and features roasted langoustines with black salsifys; glazed turbot with rosehip and *marjolaine*, and foie gras with local apples and Danish apple balsamic vinegar.

Restaurant Godt

Gothersgade 38; tel: 33 15 21 22; www.restaurant-godt.dk; Tue–Sat 6pm–midnight, closed July; €€€€

Godt means 'good', something of an understatement for this family-run, 20-seat restaurant. The cuisine is European with daily four- and five-course seasonal

Above from far left: refreshing drinks; traditional open sandwich; Japanese food is popular with the young hip crowd; asparagus with a Danish twist.

Fixed Menus
Many restaurants have fixed-price menus and the greater the number of courses, proportionately the cheaper your meal becomes. If you are on more of a budget, eat in a café where a couple of unpretentious courses will set you back 150–200dkk or try out the *pølsevogn*, sausage vans that you will find all over town. Also, bear in mind that alcohol is expensive, especially in restaurants.

Kontiki Bar
Takkelloftvej 1z
v/operahuset; tel: 40
50 90 48; open daily
until late; €.
If the stylish bar/
restaurant at the
opera house doesn't
appeal, head for this
rough-and-ready boat
just behind it. The
menu is not extensive
and changes at the
whim of the chef. Not
sophisticated but
charming – especially
on a summer evening.

Vegetarian Dining
The Danes sure do
love their meat. In a
city renowned for its
restaurants, there
are hardly any
places that cater
solely to
vegetarians. There
are several raw-food
cafes where you
can eat super-
healthy lunches, for
example the newly
opened Firefly *(see
p.119).* Some of the
city's top restaurants
will rustle up a
meat-free alternative
if given advance
notice.

menus; the wine list is mainly French. Reservations are advised.

Restaurationen
Møntergade 19; tel: 33 14 94 95;
www.restaurationen.com; Tue–Sat
6pm–9pm; €€€€
Multiple award-winning Restaurationen has survived for almost 20 years in the upper echelons of Copenhagen's competitive dining world. Its distinctive five-course fixed menu (795dkk), based on Danish, French and Italian cuisine, is revised every week, with dishes using fresh, seasonal produce. There is also a small à la carte selection. Its decor is traditional with contemporary touches.

San Giorgio
Rosenborggade 7 (near the Kultorvet);
tel: 33 12 61 20; www.san-giorgio.dk;
Mon–Sat 6–11pm; €€–€€€
Nicely decorated with white-washed walls, dark wood furniture, chandeliers, candles and crisp white tablecloths, San Giorgio offers authentic Italian cuisine that is very much more than just pizza and pasta. Three fixed menus give you a choice on price.

St Gertrude's Kloster
Hauserplads 32; tel: 33 14 66 30;
Mon–Sat 11.30am–4.30pm &
5.30pm–11pm; €€€
This lovely restaurant can be found within the atmospheric walls of a 14th-century monastery. Begin with an aperitif in the leather-book-lined library before repairing to the candlelit vault to eat. The Monastery Menu, with a faintly medieval twist, is the

most popular and is changed each month according to what is in season.

Amalienborg and Around
Le Sommelier
Bredgade 63-65; tel: 33 11 45 15;
www.lesommelier.dk; Mon–Thur
noon–2pm and 6–10pm, Fri noon–
2pm and 6–11pm, Sat 6–11pm,
Sun 6–10pm; €€€–€€€€
A charming French restaurant, Le Sommelier reputedly has the largest cellar in Denmark, offering wine by the bottle or by the glass – often cheaper than you might expect. The food is delicious (approach the *assiette tout chocolat* with an open waistband). The menu changes but expect lamb, beef, pork, duck, foie gras and fresh fish in a variety of interesting dishes.

Madklubben Bistro de Luxe
Store Kongensgade 66; tel: 33 32 32
34; www.madklubben.info; Mon–Sat
5.30–10pm; €
If you want to dine out in Copenhagen in civilised style but don't have a bottomless wallet, try this relaxed and unpretentious spot. It keeps costs low by offering a basic (but high-quality) menu, with surcharges for more luxurious items such as lobster and smoked duck.

Prices for an average three-course meal without wine:	
€€€€	over 550dkk
€€€	400–550dkk
€€	250–400dkk
€	under 250dkk

Above from far
left: wine by the
glass; presentation
is of the essence;
Noma, the only
two-starred Michelin
restaurant in
Copenhagen; a
feast for the eyes.

Slotsholmen and South of Strøget

Rio Bravo

Vester Voldgade 86; tel: 33 11 75 87;
www.riobravo.dk; Mon–Sat 11.30pm–
5am, Sun 5pm–5am; €–€€

This popular place is a favourite among
late-night revellers. It's a no-nonsense,
cowboy-style steakhouse, where even
the seats at the bar are saddles.

Slotskælderen

Fortunstræde 4; tel: 33 11 15 37;
Tue–Sat 10am–5pm; €–€€

This is a small restaurant dating from
1910 and much favoured by politicians
from the nearby parliament who enjoy
their excellent open sandwiches and
Danish menu, including home-cured
herring and home-brewed *snaps*.

Sorgenfri

Brolæggerstræde 8; tel: 33 11 58 80;
Mon–Sat 11am–9pm, Sun
noon–5pm; €

This 150-year-old *frokost* restaurant
tucked in a basement just north of
Christiansborg Castle is not posh but,
for a very Danish fast-food eaterie, it
has good *smørrebrød*, beer and *snaps*.

Christianshavn and Holmen

Era Ora

Overgaden Neden Vandet 33B;
tel: 32 54 06 93; www.era-ora.dk;
Mon–Sat lunch noon–2pm, dinner
7pm–1am (kitchen closes 10pm);
€€€–€€€€

This friendly Michelin-starred, stylish
Italian restaurant by the canal has a
calming, Italianate, beige-and-white

interior and a pretty summer courtyard. Era Ora serves innovative Italian
cuisine and is considered one of the
best restaurants in the city.

Noma

Strandgade 93, Nordatlantens
Brygghe, Christianshavn; tel: 32 96
32 97; www.noma.dk; €€€€

Noma is the stuff of legends, topping
the S.Pellegrino World's 50 Best
Restaurants list in 2010 and 2011.
Superstar chef René Redzepi takes its
inspiration, both in terms of decor and
cuisine, from Denmark, Iceland,
Greenland and the Faroe islands from
where it imports its fresh ingredients
every day. The chef conjures up dishes
such as bouillon of birch wine and
mushrooms, chickweed and egg yolk;
and reindeer and celery, woodruff and
ramson onion capers, and has earnt
two Michelin stars. Bookings are taken
up to three months in advance; com-
petition for a table is fierce.

Nørrebro

KiinKiin

Guldbergsgade 21; tel: 35 35 75 55
(for takeaways: 35 35 95 05);
www.kiin.dk; Mon–Sat 5.30–9pm;
€€€€

The name is an exhortation to 'come
and eat!', and it's hard to turn down this
rising star on the Copenhagen gourmet
scene – the first Asian restaurant in
Denmark to win a Michelin star. It
offers a daily menu of five modern Thai
courses in a lovely ambience. Also
check out its takeaway menu at a reasonable 75–95dkk per dish.

Here are our picks for some of the hottest bars and clubs in the city. There are always new places popping up – chat to friendly locals to find out about the latest 'in' spots. Many of Copenhagen's best nightspots blur the line between bar and restaurant: often when the nibbles have gone and the kitchen closes, a place will slide smoothly into 'club' mode, staying open late into the night.

Vesterbro

The Brass Monkey

Enghavevej 31; tel: 33 22 34 33; www.brassmonkey.dk; Thur–Sat 8pm–3am

The 'tiki' bar Brass Monkey comes as close as Scandinavia ever does to dubious taste. Its bartenders wear eye-watering Hawaiian shirts, and its cocktails (based on rum, rum and more rum) are served in goblets shaped like ceramic skulls, zombies and Easter-Island style heads.

Jolene

Flæsketorvet 81–5; tel: 35 85 69 60; Sun–Thur 5pm–2am, Fri–Sat 5pm–3am

This beery place in the Kødbyen district is run by two Icelandic women, who bring Iceland's characteristic eccentricity to one of Copenhagen's coolest clubs. It's loud and odd, with fleamarket decor, party-hard youngsters. Music on weekdays is described as 'alternative darksided 7 inches and tunes to watch girls cry', while at weekends DJs play hiphop, indie, pop and electronica.

Karriere Bar

Flæsketorvet 57-67; tel: 33 21 55 09; www.karrierebar.com; Thur–Sat 4pm–4am

Ouch! This experimental bar and restaurant, based in a former Vesterbro butchers' hall, is so hip it hurts. Run by artist Jeppe Hein, it's a place where art and clubbing meet. Olafur Eliasson provided the lighting when the bar first opened; now six more artists have created shining installations. Sample the house cocktails at a bar that moves slowly from side to side.

Vega Nightclub

Enghavevej 40; tel: 33 25 70 11; www.vega.dk; Fri–Sat 11pm–5am; free before 1am; concerts: charge

This huge complex of bars, clubs and music venues has everything that you require for a night out. The main-stream nightclub has wild lightshows and DJs. An impressive list of top international act, including Prince, Kylie and Bowie, have performed here.

Around Strøget & Rådhuspladsen

BrewPub

Vestergade 29; tel: 33 32 00 60; www.brewpub.dk; Mon–Thur noon–midnight, Fri–Sat noon–2am

This pub, in snug 17th-century premises near to the Rådhus, brews its own pilsner-style beers in the basement. There are usually 14 on tap, as well as a huge choice of bottled beers. True beer aficionados can get a 'tasting tray' of five draft beers, or take a tour of the brewery itself (7pm Mondays).

K Bar

Ved Stranden 20; tel: 33 91 92 22;
www.k-bar.dk; Mon–Thur 4pm–1am,
Fri–Sat 4pm–2am

Close to Højbro Plads, this teeny, tiny
Bar promotes 'København, kærlighed &
kocktails' (Copenhagen, love and cocktails). It's renowned for martinis – there
are 13 different varieties on the menu.

Mojo's

Løngangstræde 21C; tel: 33 11 64 53;
www.mojo.dk; 8pm–5am; charge

This intimate place is an exciting jazz
venue, known for its laid-back blues
and quality performers. It has live
music every night of the week, but fills
up fast: the best way to get in is to book
a table ahead of time.

Kongens Nytorv

Hviids Vinstue

Kongens Nytorv 19; tel: 33 15 10 64

Cosy, atmospheric and pub-like,
Copenhagen's oldest wine bar dates
from 1723. In winter, sit in the wood-
panelled interior; in summer, sit
outside. There is a smoking room if
you don't want to brave the elements.

Rosenborg & Around

Bibendum

Nansensgade 45; tel: 33 33 07 74;
www.bibendum.dk; Mon–Sat
4pm–midnight

Wine-lovers should head for this
pleasing bar, run by a wine importer.
There are 134 varieties to choose from,
from all over the globe; and 33 of them
are available by the glass. The
waiters/bartenders are very knowledge-
able, and the small food menu goes well
with wining: tapas is a speciality.

Nørrebro

Nørrebro Bryghus

Ryesgade 3, tel: 35 30 05 30;
Mon–Thur 11am–midnight, Fri–Sat
11am–2am

This super microbrewery has won
awards for its beers, which you can
sample at the bar or (in fine weather)
at tables on the street; but it's not all
about getting tipsy in the sunshine. The
Bryghus also offers a creative food menu
specially designed to go with the hoppy,
malty flavour of its amber brews.

Rust

Guldbergsgade 8; tel: 35 24 52 00;
www.rust.dk; Wed–Sat 9pm–5am;
over-20 in the nightclub and concerts after 11pm; charge

Rust is at the forefront of the city's
music and clubbing scene, showcasing
international DJs and live bands. It's
particularly good on rising indie/pop
stars, although bigger names, such as
Rufus Wainwright, have sung here too.
There are four bars on site, including the
Upstairs rock bar, with a smoking room.

Christianshavn

Eiffel Bar

Wildersgade 58; tel: 32 57 70 92;
daily 9am–3am

This old bar, which has been running
in its present form for 50 years, makes
no concessions to the 21st century. It's
decorated with anachronistic symbols
of Paris, and sells cheap beer to retired
sailors and local students.

**Above from far
left:** Nørrebro
Bryghus; Kirsten
Holm, owner of the
K Bar; cocktail
ingredients; out on
the town.

CREDITS

Insight Step by Step Copenhagen
Written by: Antonia Cunningham
Updated by: Fran Parnell
Series Editor: Carine Tracanelli
Edited by: Rachel Lawrence
Art Editor: Ian Spick
Map Production: APA Cartograhpy Department
Photography by: Apa/Rudy Hemmingsen/David Hall except: 4Corners 8-1, 63-1; AKG 49-3; Axel Guldsmeden 27-1, 114-2, 115-2, 121-1; Bridgeman Art Library 63-2 © Succession H Matisse/DACS 2008; Camerapress 72-1; Carlsberg 28-2, 29-1, 29-3, 29-4, 31-1; Antonia Cunningham 65-1; Design Hotels 40-1; Experimentarium 95-2, 95-3, 95-4; Front 36-3, 98-4, 98-5, 112-1, 113-1; Getty Images 11-1; Hotel 27 15-3, 27-3, 38-4, 40-2, 98-1, 98-3, 110-2, 111-1, 114-2, 116-1, 117-1, 120-1; Hotel Fox 108/109(all); iStockphoto.com 2-1, 2-2, 4-2, 8-2, 8-4, 8-7, 10-1, 12-3, 13-2, 14-2, 14-5, 16-1, 16-2, 18-1, 22-1, 23-1, 24-1, 24-2, 24-5, 44-2, 45-4, 51-1, 51-2, 53-1, 55-2, 55-3, 58-4, 67-1, 67-3, 70 (all), 74-1, 77-2, 85-3, 88-1, 89-2, 90-3, 90-4, 92-2, 100, 101, 103-1, 106, 116-2, 118-2; K-Bar 122-2, 123-1; Leonard 19-1, 26-1, 40-4, 43-3, 98-2, 98-7; Rex Features 41-2; Rust 20-2, 20-3, 21-2; SEIER+SEIER 24-4; SMK Foto 60-1, 60-2, 60-3, 60-4, 62-2, 64 (all); Superstock 80-2; Tycho Brahe Planetarium 66-2; VEGA 21-1; VisMedia 116-1, 117 (all); Wonderful Copenhagen 6-5, 10-2, 10-3, 13-3, 14-1, 14-3, 14-4, 15-1, 15-2, 16-3, 16-4, 17-1, 18-2, 18-3, 19-2, 19-3, 27-2, 28-1, 28-3, 32-2, 32-3, 36-2, 37-1, 37-4, 40-3, 43-1, 44-3, 45-5, 46 (all), 47-1, 49-1, 50-2, 59-3, 66-1, 67-2, 81-3, 97-1, 97-2, 97-4, 98-6, 102 (all), 107, 117-2, 118-1, 119-2, 120-2, 121 (all), 122-1, 123-1.
Front Cover: main image Getty Images; bottom left C.B Poulsen/Wonderful Copenhagen; bottom right Apa/Rudy Hemmingsen.

Printed by: CTPS-China

No part of this book may be reproduced, stored in a retrieval system or transmitted in any form or by any means (electronic, mechanical, photocopying, recording or otherwise), without prior written permission of Apa Publications. Brief text quotations with use of photographs are exempted for book review purposes only. Information has been obtained from sources believed to be reliable, but its accuracy and completeness, and the opinions based thereon, are not guaranteed.

CONTACTING THE EDITORS

We would appreciate it if readers would alert us to errors or outdated information by writing to us at insight@apaguide.co.uk or APA Publications, PO Box 7910, London SE1 1WE, UK.

www.insightguides.com

DISTRIBUTION

Worldwide
APA Publications GmbH & Co. Verlag KG
(Singapore branch)
7030 Ang Mo Kio Ave 5
08-65 Northstar @ AMK, Singapore 569880
Email: apasin@singnet.com.sg

UK and Ireland
Dorling Kindersley Ltd
(a Penguin Company)
80 Strand, London, WC2R 0RL, UK
Email: customerservice@dk.com

US
Ingram Publisher Services
One Ingram Blvd, PO Box 3006
La Vergne, TN 37086-1986
Email: customer.service@ingrampublisher
services.com

Australia
Universal Publishers
PO Box 307
St. Leonards NSW 1590
Email: sales@universalpublishers.com.au

New Zealand
Brown Knows Publications
11 Artesia Close, Shamrock Park
Auckland, New Zealand 2016
Email: sales@brownknows.co.nz

INDEX

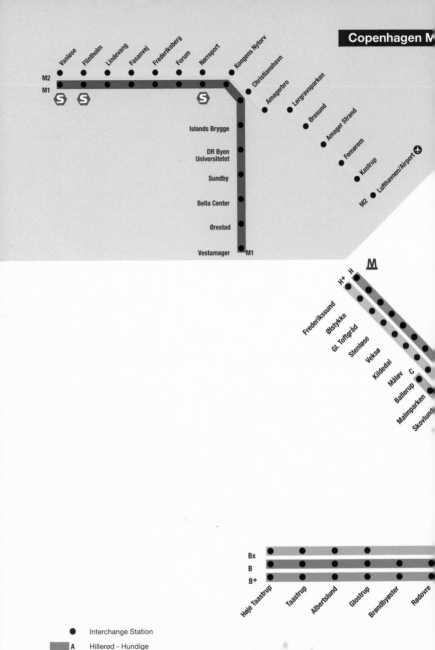

Copenhagen M

Vanløse · Flintholm · Lindevang · Fasanvej · Frederiksberg · Forum · Nørreport · Kongens Nytorv · Christianshavn · Amagerbro · Lergravsparken · Øresund · Amager Strand · Femøren · Kastrup · Lufthavnen/Airport

M2
M1

Islands Brygge
DR Byen Universitetet
Sundby
Bella Center
Ørestad
Vestamager — M1

M2 — Lufthavnen/Airport

M

H+ · H
Frederikssund · Ølstykke · Gl. Toftgård · Stenløse · Veksø · Kildedal · Måløv · C · Ballerup · Malmparken · Skovlund

Bx
B
B+
Høje Taastrup · Taastrup · Albertslund · Glostrup · Brøndbyøster · Rødovre

●		Interchange Station
A		Hillerød - Hundige
A+		Østerport - Køge
B		Holte - Høje Taastrup
B+		Holte - Høje Taastrup
Bx		Klampenborg - Høje Taastrup
C		Klampenborg - Ballerup
E		Hillerød - Køge
Ex		Hellerup - Køge
F,F+		Klampenborg - Ny Ellebjerg
H		Farum - Frederikssund
H+		Farum - Frederikssund

Copenhagen S-tog (S-train)